The Barabbas Bias

The Intersection of Faith & Politics

By

Jurgen Matthesius

Published by Meteor.land
Anaheim, CA

CONTENTS

Introduction

In a world that seems increasingly divided, where vitriol often drowns out reason and where hatred appears to overwhelm love, I believe we've been infected with what I call "the Barabbas bias." This unconscious predisposition affects how we view politics, religion, culture, and each other—often without our awareness.

You may wonder what a biblical figure from two thousand years ago has to do with the chaos we see in modern society. The answer, I believe, will transform how you understand the world around you and your place in it.

Throughout this book, I'll guide you through a revelation that has been burning in my heart for over a decade. We'll examine how politics and faith are not meant to be completely separate, but rather, exist as two streams of

God's authority—the kingly and the priestly—meant to keep each other accountable. We'll explore why humans have an inherent tendency to choose what is dark over what is light, what is guilty over what is innocent, and what is chaotic over what brings peace.

Drawing from my unique life journey—from being born in Germany to escaping communism, from youth ministry in Australia to leading a thriving multi-campus church in America—I'll share how these experiences have given me a distinctive lens through which to view our culture's deepest struggles. The global events of 2020 only further crystallized this understanding for me.

This book isn't about giving you simple answers to complex questions. Rather, it's about removing a veil that may be obscuring your vision. It's about recognizing patterns that have existed throughout human history and continue to play out in our modern world. Most importantly, it's about finding the antidote to the rage and division that threaten to tear us apart.

Whether you consider yourself politically engaged or not, whether you're a person of faith or a skeptic, this book will challenge you to reconsider how you view the world and the forces at work within it. My hope is that by understanding the Barabbas bias, you'll be equipped to recognize it in yourself and in our culture, and begin to counteract its destructive influence.

The journey ahead may be uncomfortable at times, as we confront truths about ourselves and our world that we'd rather ignore. Yet I believe it's only by facing these realities that we can begin to heal our personal and collective wounds. So I invite you to approach these pages with an open mind and heart, ready to see the world through new eyes.

Are you ready to take the red pill?

Chapter 1: The Revelation on the Plane

It began on an ordinary flight. Around 2010, I was heading from San Diego to North Carolina, settling in for a five-hour journey across the country. Our church in San Diego had been growing rapidly—perhaps too rapidly for our infrastructure at the time. We were running about 1,600 visitors every Sunday, but our structure could only effectively facilitate around 800 to 1,000. I was exhausted, stretched thin by the demands of leading a burgeoning congregation.

A coach I'd been working with had recently given me some advice that would prove life-changing, though not in the way either of us anticipated. "You need a disconnect," he told me. "Something that lets you fully detach so you can return to problem-solving and leadership refreshed." Knowing my love for art, he recommended an Adobe drawing program for my iPad—something I could use during my frequent flights to speaking engagements.

So there I was, earbuds in, worship music playing, opening the app as the plane prepared for takeoff. As I considered what to draw, I felt the Holy Spirit's gentle but clear direction: "I want you to paint the Ark of the Covenant."

Most people are familiar with the Ark from the Indiana Jones movie "Raiders of the Lost Ark"—that golden box with supernatural power. But the real Ark of the Covenant was far more significant than any Hollywood portrayal. It was the physical manifestation of God's presence among the Israelites, a sacred vessel described in precise detail in the book of Exodus.

I opened my Bible and began reading about its dimensions and design. The Ark was made of acacia wood, overlaid with pure gold inside and out. It had a special trim around it and rings for the carrying poles. On top of the Ark was the mercy seat, with two cherubim fashioned from a single piece of gold, their wings touching as they faced one another.

As I began to draw with my stylus, carefully recreating this sacred object, I felt an unusual sense of purpose. This wasn't just an artistic exercise—something deeper was happening. Between the cherubim was where God's Shekinah glory would dwell. God had told Moses, "There I will meet with you, and from above the mercy seat, from between the two cherubim that are on the ark of the testimony, I will speak with you."

The mercy seat itself held profound significance. Once a year, on Yom Kippur (the Day of Atonement), the high priest would select a perfect lamb. He would lean on it, confessing the sins of the nation of Israel, then sacrifice this innocent creature. Taking the blood, he would enter behind the veil into the Holy of Holies—a place only accessible this one day each year—and sprinkle the blood on the mercy seat.

Why? Because inside the Ark were three items: the tablets of the Ten Commandments, Aaron's rod that budded, and a pot of manna. These three elements represented the law we had broken, the leadership we had rejected, and the provision we had disdained. They were, in essence, three judgments against humanity. But when the blood covered the mercy seat, God would no longer see these judgments. The blood blinds the eyes of God intentionally—He cannot see your sin or mine when we're under the blood.

I was engrossed in these thoughts as I completed my drawing of the Ark. Then I felt another prompting: "Add a mist to represent My glory." Using a beautiful effect in the app, I created a misty glow between the cherubim, representing God's presence.

And that's when everything changed.

As I looked at my completed drawing, the Holy Spirit gave me a sudden revelation. I saw the two cherubim—head and wings on each side—with the glory of God between them. In an instant, this image transformed in my mind to another scene: two thieves on crosses, with Christ in the center.

"Go to Isaiah 14 and Ezekiel 28," the Holy Spirit urged—the two passages that speak about Lucifer. The name Lucifer means "light bearer" or "the shining one." He became Satan (which means "accuser") through his rebellion against God. In these passages, Lucifer is described as "the anointed cherub who covers." Covers what? The mercy seat of heaven.

Everything Moses built on earth was according to the pattern God showed him in heaven. The book of Hebrews tells us these earthly things were shadows and types of a heavenly reality. I suddenly understood that Lucifer was the cherub who broke away from his position covering the heavenly mercy seat.

What was meant to be a simple five-hour flight turned into a profound spiritual journey as God began to show me a pattern that runs throughout Scripture—a pattern revealing something fundamental about the human condition and our relationship with God.

The revelation continued as God took me to the scene of Christ's crucifixion. Jesus hanging between two thieves—one who mocked him and perished, the other who recognized him and found paradise. But this wasn't the only place this pattern appeared.

In Genesis, Joseph—a type of Christ—was thrown into prison where he encountered two men from Pharaoh's court: a butler and a baker. The butler's job was to put red wine (symbolizing blood) into the king's hand. The baker provided bread (symbolizing God's word). Both had dreams that Joseph interpreted. The butler would be restored to his position in three days; the baker would be executed.

The birds of the air came down and ate the bread from the baker's baskets—the same imagery Jesus uses in the parable of the sower, where birds represent Satan snatching away the word of God. The baker had no respect for God's word and allowed the enemy to take it. Meanwhile, the red wine in the butler's cup represented the blood of the New Covenant.

One prisoner went to death; the other to life. Just as with the two thieves on the crosses beside Jesus. But the pattern takes an intriguing turn when we come to the trial of Jesus before Pontius Pilate.

Instead of Jesus being in the center, Pilate stands in the middle as judge. God is the judge of the earth, Pilate stands in His (God) position and brings forward the two men: Jesus and Barabbas. What most people don't realize—and what many early Bible translators actually removed because they thought it inappropriate—is that Barabbas's full name, according to Matthew's gospel and the writings of Josephus, was Jesus Barabbas.

In Hebrew, "Bar" means "son of," and "Abbas" means "father." So on that fateful day, Pilate presented two men with virtually identical names: Jesus, the Son of the Father, who was sinless and blameless; and Jesus Barabbas, also Jesus, "son of the father," but he was guilty of insurrection, rebellion, and murder—the very crimes that caused Lucifer to be cast out of heaven.

Pilate expected the crowd to choose the innocent healer over the dangerous criminal. Yet inexplicably, they shouted, "Release Barabbas! Crucify Jesus!" This baffling choice reveals what I call "the Barabbas bias"—an inherent tendency in unregenerate human nature to choose what is corrupt over what is pure, what is rebellious over what is righteous.

This fits and fulfills 'another' pattern in scripture, that of the two goats. In Leviticus 16 Moses is giving instructions around the most sacred day in the Jewish calendar "The Day of Atonement" (also known as Yom Kippur) He commands Aaron to bring two identical male goats, they are to be presented before the LORD at the tabernacle of meeting. Aaron is to then cast lots for them, one will be chosen as the 'sin offering' and the other is to be released as the scapegoat into the wilderness to Azazel (Another name for satan).

The one chosen to be the sin offering, is sacrificed and its blood taken by the high priest directly into the Holy of Holies where it is to then be sprinkled upon the mercy seat of the Ark of the testimony. Atoning for the sins of Israel. Once Aaron has finished atoning for the Holy Place, the tabernacle of meeting and the altar he is to bring the other goat. He is now instructed to 'lay his hands' upon the head of the other goat and confess the sin and iniquity of the nation of Israel and then that goat is to be released into the wilderness by the hand of a suitable man. This goat carries the sin and judgment of God's people upon itself into the wilderness. This is BarAbbas. He bears the iniquity of Lucifer, the rebellious one, who split heaven, causing one third of the holy angels to rebel and lose their place. Isn't it interesting that the devil often depicts himself as a Goat!

These patterns are so rich and prevalent throughout scripture. Abraham (Father of Multitudes) is to sacrifice his only begotten son (Isaac) out of obedience and love for God. Again we see the pattern that instead of Isaac being sacrificed, a Ram caught in the thicket by its horns is sacrificed while Isaac is freed.

Five hours of divine revelation left me shaken and transformed. I realized I had been given a profound insight into the human condition—one that explains so much about our world, our politics, and our personal struggles. This wasn't just about ancient history; it was about the invisible forces still shaping our world today.

In the years following that flight, I continued to see this pattern play out in our culture, in politics, and in the daily struggles we all face. The revelation became even more relevant during the turmoil of 2020, as the world faced a global pandemic, social unrest, and unprecedented division.

This bias—this unconscious preference for darkness over light—is something we all battle with. It's part of our fallen nature. But recognizing it is the first step to overcoming it. Like Neo in "The Matrix," we must choose to take the red pill—to see the reality behind the illusion.

As you journey through this book, I invite you to look for this pattern in your own life and in the world around you. When we understand the Barabbas bias, we can begin to counter it with the only true antidote: the transformative power of God's love.

Implementation: Recognizing Divine Patterns in Your Everyday Life

1. **Practice pattern recognition:** Set aside time each day to read Scripture and look for recurring themes, characters, or situations. Journal what you find.
2. **Connect biblical patterns to current events:** The next time you read or watch the news, ask yourself if you can see any of the biblical patterns we've discussed playing out in our world today.

3. **Examine your own preferences:** In what areas of your life might you be unconsciously choosing "Barabbas" over "Jesus"? Where might you be preferring what is comfortable but corrupt over what is challenging but pure?
4. **Create your own visual reminders:** Consider creating a simple drawing or symbol that represents a truth God has revealed to you. Place it somewhere visible as a daily reminder.
5. **Invite divine revelation:** Begin each day asking God to open your eyes to see the patterns and meanings in everyday circumstances. You might be surprised at what He shows you through ordinary moments.

Chapter 2: My Journey: From Germany to God's Purpose

I was born in Southern Germany, in a small town called Tuttlingen at the bottom of the Black Forest. My name itself—Jürgen—reflects these Germanic roots, though it's often mispronounced. In German, the "J" sounds like a "Y," so it's pronounced "Yurgen," not "Jurgen." This detail may seem minor, but our names, like our origins, carry significance that shapes our stories in ways we can't always predict.

I was just a little over two years old, my mother pregnant with my younger brother, when my family's trajectory changed dramatically. That winter in Germany was particularly severe, with heavy snowfall blanketing the region for nearly three months. My father was a Fliesenleger—a German tiler who did bathrooms, kitchens, and outdoor patios. The extreme winter made it impossible for him to reach his job sites, wiping out 90 percent of his work.

With no income, he couldn't afford to keep oil in our heater. Our little apartment grew colder as the winter deepened. Someone suggested to him, "You should think about going to Australia. You can work all year round there—they don't have snow." For a man with a young family and another child on the way, this suggestion was lifeline. That's how we ended up immigrating to Australia, where I would spend my formative years.

But there's a deeper story behind our move, one rooted in my father's harrowing experiences in post-World War II Germany. After the war, Europe was divided, with a line cutting right through the heart of Germany. The eastern portion fell under the control of the USSR, becoming part of the communist bloc, while the western side remained in the free world under capitalism. My father had no say in which side of this division he was born on. He found himself in East Germany, effectively living not in a country but in a prison.

He would tell me stories about how, to visit a friend in the next town over, he would have to stop at checkpoints, present papers, and endure interrogations: "Who are you visiting? What will you be talking about? Will you be discussing the government or planning acts of rebellion? What time will you return?" There was no freedom of movement or expression.

At 18, like all young men, he was conscripted into military service. After training, they stationed him as a guard on the Berlin Wall. The authorities told him, "You're guarding this wall because those capitalists on the West want to break in. They want the free sausages we provide every Tuesday and the free bread we distribute on Thursdays—even if it is a bit stale."

The reality, of course, was exactly the opposite. No one was trying to break into East Germany. People were desperately trying to escape. My father realized this fully when he was ordered to shoot a defector attempting to flee to West Germany. He refused. Later, his partner reported him for commenting that the West German uniforms looked superior to their East German counterparts—a sign of "disloyalty" to the regime.

For these "offenses," my father was imprisoned in a concentration camp for 26 months. When he was finally released, he was determined never to live under communist rule again. That night, drawing on his knowledge as a former wall guard, he made a desperate escape attempt. He ran across a minefield—the least guarded but most dangerous section of the border—and fought through razor wire, suffering scars that he would carry for the rest of his life.

Having made it to West Germany, he was still afraid. Without a passport, he feared being deported back to East Germany if he tried to cross into Switzerland or France. So he went as far away as possible within West Germany, to Tuttlingen, where I was eventually born. Even there, he lived with constant anxiety that the East German authorities might find him.

This history I carried with me, even if I didn't fully understand it as a child. When we moved to Australia, I grew up as any other kid might, but with this background informing my perspective in ways I wouldn't fully comprehend until much later.

As an 18-year-old in Australia, I was like many young men—trying to figure out who I was and what I wanted to do with my life. I fell in love with surfing and thought perhaps I could make a career in the surfing industry or even become a professional surfer. I entered competitions and was building my skills, imagining a future riding waves.

Then something happened that would completely redirect my path. Through a Jesus program, I had an encounter with Christ that changed everything. My life's trajectory shifted as dramatically as when my family had moved from Germany to Australia, but this time the change was internal, spiritual, and entirely transformative.

This conversion experience planted the seeds for what would eventually become Awaken Church. But the path from that moment to leading a thriving multi-campus church wasn't direct or immediate. Like many aspects of God's work in our lives, it unfolded over time, through seasons of preparation that seemed unrelated to my ultimate calling.

My wife and I spent the first fifteen years of our marriage in youth ministry. The initial seven years were in New Zealand, followed by another seven years at a great church on Sydney's Northern beaches in Australia. During that second period, we saw the youth group grow from about 50 kids to over 1,000. We were active in high schools, running programs and connecting with young people where they were.

Youth ministry suited my personality perfectly. I often tell people that being a youth pastor is the "Peter Pan of ministry"—you never have to grow up. You get to be edgy, push boundaries, and do things that might get you arrested as a senior pastor but give you "street cred" with teenagers.

We were known as the radical youth ministry. We would “borrow” meal trays from McDonalds, drill a hole in it and then attach a high tensile steel cable, attaching it to the back of a truck and then have our “PULSE” Man sit in it and see what speed we could get it up to before he would come flying off! One time we got it up to 70 KM/H before “Pulse” got airborne and flew off into the lantana bushes! We would always have a fire extinguisher present, (actual fire was not necessary) where we would douse him with fire after each stunt, to show that we were practicing ‘safety!’ To the very bored and very spoiled teenagers we were the coolest youth group around!

Our youth ministry was called "Pulse" (P-U-L-S-E), and we created a character called "Pulse Man." He wore a Superman outfit with the "S" changed to a "P" and a John Travolta mask. The teenager who played Pulse Man wanted to be a stuntman, so we'd film him doing increasingly outrageous stunts.

In one memorable incident, he filled a mall fountain with detergent until it overflowed, then dove in wearing goggles and flippers. He got arrested by security, but the stunt only amplified our reputation. Another time, he rode his BMX bike off a cliff into a blowhole during high surf—a dangerous stunt, people would JUMP into the blowhole, but nobody had ever ridden a BMX bike into it. In this stunt he barely had enough speed and momentum to clear the rock ledge below. But miraculously he made it, but the bike didn't. It hit the rock ledge, but thank God he landed in the water, where he surfaced still clutching the handlebars of the now disintegrated BMX bike!

After each stunt, we'd play our jingle: "Yeah, he's Pulse Man! He can do anything you can't! He's Pulse Man!" The following Friday, 250 students would show up, with Pulse Man signing autographs. The 'pushing the envelope' was what it took to inspire YOUTH to see Christ as both radical and relevant! Behind the antics, we had incredible praise and worship, powerful prayer meetings, inspirational preaching, lots of humor, prizes, giveaways and every week we would see lots of young people getting saved.

I loved being a little edgy, "fun and powerful" was our motto.. You can't do that stuff as a senior pastor. As the youth pastor, you're pushing boundaries; as the senior pastor, you're defining them. So when my senior pastor sat down with me after seven years and asked, "Have you ever thought that there might be a church in you?" I was conflicted. I had considered it but was reluctant to leave the fun and freedom of youth ministry.

Nevertheless, in 2005, my wife and I moved to San Diego and started what would become Awaken Church. God initially gave me a vision of one church in four locations. In just 19 years, that expanded to one church in ten locations, with plans for two more, spanning four different states—San Diego, California; Boise, Idaho; Salt Lake City, Utah; and Seattle, Washington—with West Palm Beach, Florida, on the horizon.

By 2020, we had grown to about 5,000 members across five campuses. Then came what I consider a pivotal testing period. The year 2020 itself is significant numerically—adding up to 40, which in the Bible consistently represents testing. Moses was tested in the wilderness for 40 years, Jesus was tested by the devil for 40 days, the children of Israel wandered 40 years, and Noah endured the flood for 40 days and 40 nights.

Additionally, the term "20/20" in optometry represents perfect vision, but as any eye doctor will tell you, perfect 20/20 vision doesn't really exist—except in hindsight. This seemed prophetic, suggesting that what we would experience in 2020—COVID-19, Black Lives Matter protests, riots, and global shutdowns—wouldn't make sense until we looked back at it.

When the pandemic hit, we initially complied with lockdown orders for about six weeks, observing social distancing and mask mandates like most churches. But something inside me began to react strongly against what I perceived as government overreach. I believe this reaction was partly influenced by my family history.

Recent scientific studies have shown that trauma can be imprinted on DNA. Researchers can determine with 1% accuracy whether someone had a relative who experienced the Holocaust through DNA testing. In our church, we have a young woman who could never lose weight despite numerous attempts. Her doctor discovered her thyroid was completely shut down—a condition typically seen only in Holocaust survivors. The explanation? Her grandmother was a Holocaust survivor, and the body's adaptation to conserve energy during extreme starvation had been passed down genetically.

Similarly, I believe my father's experiences in East Germany—the oppression, imprisonment, and desperate escape—were somehow encoded in my spiritual and psychological DNA. When government mandates began restricting church gatherings while allowing businesses like Walmart and Home Depot to operate, something in me rebelled. I had what I can only describe as an "allergic reaction" to what felt like government tyranny disguised as public health measures.

Against considerable opposition, I reopened our church. We accumulated 48 ten-thousand-dollar fines that we refused to pay. We made the front page of newspapers and were labeled "conspiracy theorists," "super-spreaders," and "grandma killers" by critics—including, sadly, by many fellow pastors who distanced themselves from us.

Yet I stood firm in my conviction. I often tell people, "The difference between a conspiracy theorist and a prophet is about five to six months." As time passed, many of our positions were validated: social distancing guidelines were arbitrary, mask efficacy was overstated, and certain treatments like ivermectin (which we obtained from Mexico for our congregants) proved effective. Despite thousands in our church contracting COVID, we had zero deaths—largely because we prevented them from receiving treatments like Remdesivir that many medical professionals quietly called "Run-Death-Is-Near" for its side effects.

This period of standing against the tide, despite intense criticism, brought tremendous growth. Our church doubled from 5,000 to 10,000 members by the end of 2021. It also rekindled my determination to finally complete this book on the Barabbas bias—a revelation that helps explain why masses of people often choose destructive paths even when better alternatives are clearly available.

My journey from a small German town to leading a thriving American church spanning multiple states has been anything but conventional. Looking back, I can see how every part of it—from my father's escape from totalitarianism to my years as an unconventional youth pastor to our stance during COVID—has shaped my understanding of human nature, spiritual warfare, and the perpetual choice we face between truth and deception, freedom and bondage, Christ and Barabbas.

Implementation: Finding God's Purpose Within Your Personal History

1. **Examine your family history:** Take time to document your family's story, paying special attention to patterns of resilience, faith, and overcoming adversity. How might these experiences have shaped your own responses to challenges?

2. **Identify your "East Germany moments":** What systems or situations have you felt instinctively opposed to, even when others accepted them? These reactions might reveal important aspects of your calling.
3. **Recognize divine preparation:** List the seemingly unrelated skills and experiences from different seasons of your life. How might God be weaving these together for your current purpose?
4. **Honor your name and origin:** Research the meaning of your name and the history of your birthplace or ancestral homeland. These can provide insights into your identity and purpose.
5. **Find purpose in opposition:** If you've faced criticism for standing on conviction, don't waste that experience. How can your stance against the tide become part of your testimony and strengthen others?

Chapter 3: The Inherent Bias of Human Nature

The scene is etched in our collective consciousness. Pontius Pilate, caught between political expediency and his own conscience, stands before a jeering crowd. His wife has sent him an urgent message: "Have nothing to do with that innocent man." Pilate, sensing the mob's bloodlust but reluctant to condemn a man he finds faultless, attempts a strategic maneuver.

"It is your custom that I release one prisoner to you at Passover," he announces. "Whom do you want me to release: Jesus Barabbas, or Jesus who is called the Christ?"

The choice seems obvious. On one side stands Jesus of Nazareth—a healer, teacher, and miracle-worker who has done nothing but good. On the other stands Barabbas—described in scripture as a notorious prisoner, an insurrectionist, and a murderer. Surely the crowd will choose the innocent man over the criminal.

But something profound and disturbing happens. The crowd, with one voice, shouts: "Release Barabbas!"

Pilate, visibly perplexed, asks: "What shall I do, then, with Jesus who is called the Christ?"

The response comes back with chilling unanimity: "Crucify him!"

This moment reveals something fundamental about human nature—something I call the Barabbas bias. It's an inherent tendency in our unregenerate state to choose what is corrupt over what is pure, what is rebellious over what is righteous, what is destructive over what brings life.

What makes this bias even more remarkable is a detail that many Bible translations omit. If you look at the earliest manuscripts of Matthew's Gospel (Matthew 27:16-17), and the historical writings of Josephus, you'll discover something startling: Barabbas's full name was Jesus Barabbas.

Many early translators, uncomfortable with the idea that such a villain would share the same name as Christ, simply dropped the first name. But the inclusion of this detail adds profound significance to the scene. Pilate wasn't just presenting two random men—he was presenting two men with virtually identical names.

The 'Type' could not be fulfilled more clearly. Forgive me for repeating this point, In Hebrew, "Bar" means "son of," and "Abbas" means "father." So on that fateful day, Pilate presented two men with the same first name, Jesus. While both also bore the title Bar Abbas "son of the father"—one however was divine and sinless, while the other utterly corrupt, unrepentant and guilty.

Jesus, the Son of the Father, sinless, spotless, and blameless.

Jesus Barabbas, son of the father, guilty of insurrection, rebellion, and murder.

These crimes are significant because they mirror the very offenses that caused Lucifer to be cast out of heaven. BarAbbas was the embodiment of Lucifer's rebellion. Jesus Christ was the embodiment of God the father and all that is pure, righteous and holy. The crowd, faced with these two figures, chose the one who embodied the qualities of the fallen angel over the one who embodied the nature of God.

This wasn't just a historical anomaly. It was a revelation of something embedded in human nature—a bias that continues to shape our choices today, often without our conscious awareness.

Why would people choose Barabbas over Jesus? The answer lies in our fallen nature. When we are not born again, when the spirit of truth hasn't transformed our hearts, we unconsciously align with rebellion against God. The Bible makes this clear when it says that "the mind governed by the flesh is hostile to God; it does not submit to God's law, nor can it do so" (Romans 8:7).

This bias finds its ultimate fulfillment in what the Bible calls "the man of sin," the Antichrist, who will gather all those who do not 'love the truth' and reject the 'word of God' thus refusing to be born again, into a final rebellion against God. But we don't need to look to end-times prophecy to see this bias at work. It manifests in countless ways in our everyday decisions and cultural preferences.

Consider how our unregenerate culture often responds to moral issues. When discussing the death penalty for the most heinous criminals—serial killers who have committed unimaginable atrocities—many will argue that execution is inhumane, regardless of the crimes committed. Yet these same voices often advocate for abortion rights, even supporting late-term procedures.

Do you see the pattern? There is a willingness to slaughter what is innocent while pardoning what is guilty. This is the Barabbas bias in action.

We witness this in international responses to terrorism as well. When Islamic extremists commit acts of violence, certain media outlets and political figures rush to defend Islam rather than condemn the atrocity. After an attack where dozens are injured or killed, the focus quickly shifts to preventing "Islamophobia" rather than addressing the ideology that motivated the violence.

Again, we see protection of the guilty and persecution of the innocent—a pattern that reflects the crowd's choice of Barabbas over Jesus.

The Barabbas bias also explains much of the irrational hatred directed at certain public figures who stand for traditional values or conservative principles. During the Trump presidency, for example, the vitriol reached levels that couldn't be explained by mere political disagreement. People who couldn't articulate a single specific policy objection nonetheless felt intense hatred toward him.

When asked what they hate about such figures, many can't provide concrete examples: "He's committed crimes!" "What crimes?" "So many!" "Name one." "He's just... bad!" This visceral, irrational response points to something deeper than political disagreement—it's a spiritual alignment with rebellion against divine order.

Conversely, figures who embody corruption, deception, and self-enrichment often receive protection and adoration from the same voices. The Biden family laptop controversy provides a telling example. Despite clear evidence of influence-peddling and corruption, many media outlets and political figures dismissed it as "Russian disinformation," only to quietly acknowledge its authenticity later when the political moment had passed.

The contrast couldn't be clearer: hatred for a leader who sacrificed financially to serve his country versus protection for those who leveraged power for personal gain. This isn't about partisan politics—it's about recognizing a spiritual pattern that transcends political affiliation.

The Bible tells us that "the whole world lies in the power of the evil one" (1 John 5:19). This influence manifests in our unconscious preferences and reactions. We don't understand why we rage against certain things or why we feel such animosity toward certain people. This isn't just about politics or personal preference—it's about a spiritual bias that pulls us toward rebellion and away from divine order.

The Barabbas bias also explains why social movements that begin with seemingly noble intentions often devolve into destructive chaos. Consider recent justice movements that started with legitimate concerns but quickly descended into rioting, looting, and violence. The spirit behind such devolution isn't justice but chaos—the same rebellious spirit embodied by Barabbas.

This bias affects our personal lives too. Why do we often choose what we know will harm us over what will heal us? Why do addictions hold such power? Why do destructive relationships seem more alluring than healthy ones? The Barabbas bias inclines us toward what destroys rather than what builds up.

Jesus understood this aspect of human nature perfectly. He knew that "the Son of Man must suffer many things and be rejected" (Mark 8:31). When Peter pulled Jesus aside and insisted this would never happen, Jesus rebuked him sharply: "Get behind me, Satan! You do not have in mind the concerns of God, but merely human concerns" (Mark 8:33).

Jesus knew the Barabbas bias would lead to his rejection and crucifixion. He understood that fallen humanity would choose a murderer over the Prince of Peace, rebellion over redemption.

This bias reaches all the way back to the first murder recorded in Scripture—when Cain killed Abel. These brothers represent two approaches to God: human effort versus divine provision. Cain brought "an offering of the fruit of the ground" (Genesis 4:3), representing human works and self-effort. Abel brought "of the firstborn of his flock" (Genesis 4:4), representing faith in a sacrifice he didn't produce himself.

When God accepted Abel's offering but rejected Cain's, Cain became enraged—not at himself for bringing an inadequate offering, but at his brother who had done right. This pattern continues throughout history: those who try to earn God's favor through self-effort often become enraged at those who simply receive it through faith.

The names themselves reveal prophetic significance. "Cain" means "acquired spear," while "Abel" combines "Ab" (father) and "El" (God). It's a prophetic picture: the world (represented by Cain) would use an acquired spear to murder the representation of Father God (Abel), who brought an innocent lamb to be sacrificed.

These two spirits—self-effort versus received grace, rebellion versus submission, pride versus humility—continue to operate in our world. And until we are born again, we naturally align with the wrong side.

This is precisely why Jesus insisted to Nicodemus: "Very truly I tell you, no one can see the kingdom of God unless they are born again" (John 3:3). Notice the language: not just "enter" the kingdom, but "see" it. Without spiritual rebirth, we remain blind to divine reality, unconsciously choosing Barabbas over Jesus, rebellion over redemption, death over life.

How is one 'born again?'

How were you born the first time? A seed from your father was received in the inner place, the womb of your mother. Instantly life began and after 40 weeks (Trial/tribulation) you were born. To be 'born again' you must receive the 'seed' of God. Jesus Christ. The word. (See John 1:1) When you receive His word into your inner place, your heart you are born again and you become a child of God, a child of heaven, with everlasting life.

The Barabbas bias is like a veil over our spiritual eyes. It's a predisposition that affects our perceptions, preferences, and choices without our awareness. It's why Jesus taught that we need not just moral improvement but complete spiritual transformation—a new birth that changes our very nature.

When we understand this bias, political and cultural conflicts make more sense. We're not just witnessing different policy preferences; we're seeing the manifestation of a spiritual divide as old as humanity itself. It's the difference between those who have been born again, receiving a new nature aligned with God's kingdom, and those who remain in their natural state, unconsciously aligned with rebellion.

This doesn't mean every political position can be neatly categorized as "of God" or "of Satan." Human affairs are complex, and sincere believers can disagree on specific policies or approaches. But understanding the Barabbas bias helps us recognize when movements, ideologies, or leaders embody the spirit of rebellion rather than the spirit of truth.

The good news is that this bias isn't our destiny. Unlike genetic traits we can't change, this spiritual predisposition can be transformed through the new birth Jesus described. When we are born again, we receive a new nature that aligns with God's kingdom rather than rebellion against it. We begin to see with new eyes, recognize the patterns of heaven versus the patterns of hell, and instinctively choose life over death.

Understanding the Barabbas bias is the first step toward overcoming it. Like Neo in "The Matrix" who took the red pill, we must first recognize the reality we've been blind to before we can be freed from it. Once we see this bias at work—in our culture, our politics, and our own hearts—we can begin the journey toward transformation.

Implementation: Identifying the Barabbas Bias in Modern Culture and in Yourself

1. **Media discernment practice:** Select a major news story being covered by multiple outlets. Note how different sources report on the same events. Which coverage seems to protect the guilty or attack the innocent? Which aligns with biblical values of truth and justice?
2. **Personal bias inventory:** Reflect on your gut reactions to public figures, movements, or ideas. Are there people or perspectives you irrationally dislike? Consider whether these reactions might stem from the Barabbas bias rather than reasoned evaluation.
3. **Scripture contrast study:** Create two columns in your journal. In one, list biblical characteristics of

God's kingdom (love, joy, peace, patience, etc.). In the other, list characteristics of rebellion (pride, chaos, division, accusation). Use this framework to evaluate cultural movements and your own inclinations.

4. **Decision awareness:** For one week, pause before making significant choices and ask: "Am I choosing this because it's truly good, or because it appeals to my unregenerate nature?" Look for patterns in your decision-making.
5. **Rebellion-to-submission practice:** Identify one area where you've been resistant to God's authority. It might be a commandment you've rationalized away, a conviction you've ignored, or an attitude you've justified. Commit to a specific act of submission in this area as a practical step toward countering the Barabbas bias in your life.

Chapter 4: Patterns Through Scripture

God speaks through patterns. Throughout scripture, we find recurring motifs and parallels that reveal His consistent message across generations. These aren't coincidences but divine echoes—deliberate repetitions designed to emphasize eternal truths. When we recognize these patterns, scripture transforms from a collection of isolated stories into a magnificent tapestry where each thread connects to create a cohesive picture of redemption.

In theological study, there's a principle called the Law of First Mentions. This principle states that the first occurrence of a word, phrase, or concept in scripture establishes a pattern that carries forward, developing and deepening throughout the Bible. By tracing these patterns, we gain profound insights into God's character and plan.

Let's explore three powerful scriptural patterns that illuminate the Barabbas bias and help us understand the spiritual warfare happening in our world today.

The first pattern appears in the story of Joseph. Though most Christians are familiar with Joseph's colorful coat and his rise from prisoner to prime minister of Egypt, few notice how his prison experience foreshadows Christ's crucifixion.

Joseph is a clear "type" or foreshadowing of Christ throughout Genesis. Like Jesus, he was rejected by his brothers, sold for pieces of silver, falsely accused of a crime he didn't commit, and went into what the Bible symbolically treats as "death" when he was thrown into prison. But the parallels grow even more specific during his imprisonment.

While Joseph was in prison, two officials from Pharaoh's court were also imprisoned—the butler and the baker. Both men had troubling dreams, which Joseph offered to interpret through God's wisdom. The butler described his dream first: "In my dream, there were three vine branches above my head. I squeezed the grapes into Pharaoh's cup and placed it in his hand."

Joseph's interpretation was favorable: "The three branches represent three days. Within three days, Pharaoh will restore you to your position, and you will once again place the cup in his hand."

Encouraged by this positive interpretation, the baker shared his dream: "I had three baskets on my head, and birds came down and ate the bread from the baskets."

Joseph's interpretation for the baker was grim: "Within three days, you will be beheaded and executed."

This prison scene establishes a vital pattern. The butler, who handled the cup of red wine (representing the blood of Christ), was restored to life and position. The baker, who carried bread (representing the Word of God) but allowed birds (representing Satan) to consume it, was condemned to death.

Three days later, exactly as Joseph predicted, the butler was restored to his position, and the baker was executed. One went to life; one went to death. And between them stood Joseph, a type of Christ, determining their destinies.

This pattern reappears at the crucifixion, where Jesus hangs between two thieves. One thief mocks Jesus: "If you are the Son of God, save yourself and us!" The other rebukes the first thief, acknowledging their guilt and

Jesus's innocence: "We are punished justly, for we are getting what our deeds deserve. But this man has done nothing wrong." Then, turning to Jesus, he says, "Lord, remember me when you come into your kingdom."

Jesus responds with one of scripture's most beautiful promises: "Truly I tell you, today you will be with me in paradise."

Again, we see the pattern: one goes to death, one goes to eternal life, and between them is Christ. But something fascinating happens when we come to the trial before Pilate. The pattern shifts.

Instead of Jesus being in the center position, Pontius Pilate stands in the middle. He stands in the place of a judge, God's position over the earth and over men. To his left stands Jesus, the Son of God. To his right stands Jesus Barabbas. Again both bearing the same first name, and both are "son of the father"—one divine, one corrupt.

The pattern is reversed because this scene represents humanity's choice rather than God's judgment. When humans make the choice, we consistently select rebellion over redemption, Barabbas over Jesus, unless our hearts have been transformed by divine grace.

A second crucial pattern appears in the story of Cain and Abel, the first murder in human history. This pattern reveals the root of the Barabbas bias and its manifestation in human hatred.

Cain and Abel represent two approaches to God. Cain brought "an offering of the fruit of the ground"—something he had cultivated through his own effort. This represents the Old Testament principle: if you observe the commandments, if you keep the laws, if you obey the statutes, then God will bless you. It's a works-based approach to righteousness.

Abel, in contrast, brought "a firstborn lamb from his flock"—something he didn't produce himself. This represents the New Testament principle of grace: we cannot produce our own righteousness, but must rely on the sacrifice of an innocent lamb.

God accepted Abel's offering but rejected Cain's, revealing that human effort can never produce the righteousness God requires. This truth is at the heart of the gospel: "For it is by grace you have been saved, through faith—and this is not from yourselves, it is the gift of God—not by works, so that no one can boast" (Ephesians 2:8-9).

Cain's reaction to this rejection reveals something profound about human nature. Rather than adjusting his approach to align with God's standard, he became enraged—not at God who rejected his offering, but at his brother who had done right.

This pattern of hatred toward those who have received God's approval through faith continues throughout human history. Those who try to establish their own righteousness often despise those who receive righteousness as a gift through faith.

What's particularly enlightening about this story are the names themselves. Abel's name derives from two Hebrew root words: "Ab" (father) and "El" (God), prophetically pointing to Father God. Cain's name means "acquired spear." It's a prophetic picture: the world (represented by Cain) would use an acquired spear to murder the representation of Father God (Abel), who brought an innocent lamb to be sacrificed.

When God confronts Cain about Abel's murder, He asks, "Where is your brother?" Cain's response is telling: "Am I my brother's keeper?" This is the language of someone who has rejected divine love and responsibility toward others. God then says something remarkable: "What have you done? The voice of your brother's blood cries out to Me from the ground."

This introduces a third crucial pattern: blood that cries out. Abel's innocent blood cried out to God for justice. Throughout scripture, blood has a voice—it speaks, it cries, it testifies.

This pattern finds its ultimate fulfillment in Christ. Hebrews 12:24 tells us that we have come "to Jesus the mediator of a new covenant, and to the sprinkled blood that speaks a better word than the blood of Abel."

Abel's blood cried out for justice. Jesus's blood cries out for mercy.

This is why Jesus had to suffer before His crucifixion. He could have died by any means, but He chose the most excruciating form of execution known to humanity. He was whipped and scourged, with the Shroud of Turin revealing over 326 lash marks on His body. Historians estimate there would have been no flesh left on His back.

He wore a crown of thorns—thorns representing the curse that came when God cursed the earth. Jesus took the crown of the curse to break the curse. But most importantly, His suffering elevated the frequency of His blood so that when He ascended to heaven as our High

Priest, His blood on the mercy seat of heaven would cry out with such power that God could hear nothing else.

Satan is called "the accuser of the brethren" who accuses us before God day and night: "You can't bless this person, God. Look at their thoughts, their actions, their failures." But Jesus's blood on the mercy seat drowns out these accusations with one word: "Justice." Not justice in the sense of punishment, but in the sense of "what Adam ruined, I have restored. Justice has been served—I died in their place."

These three patterns—the choice between life and death, the hatred of faith by works, and the blood that cries out—converge to help us understand both the Barabbas bias and its antidote. The bias stems from our fallen nature, which naturally aligns with rebellion against God. The antidote is the blood of Jesus, which transforms our nature through the new birth.

Understanding these biblical patterns equips us to recognize the same dynamics playing out in our world today. When we see hatred directed at those who stand for righteousness, we're witnessing Cain's rage against Abel. When we see masses choosing corrupt leadership over righteous leadership, we're seeing the crowd choosing Barabbas over Jesus. When we feel condemned by our failures, we need to remember the blood that speaks a better word than Abel's.

These patterns aren't merely historical; they're prophetic. They reveal the spiritual forces at work behind current events. The Bible says in Ecclesiastes that "what has been will be again, what has been done will be done again; there is nothing new under the sun." History operates in cycles, especially in the Jewish understanding of time.

The Jewish calendar is based on 360 days, forming a circle (360 degrees), while our Gregorian calendar is linear. This reflects two different conceptions of time: cyclic versus linear. The Jewish perspective recognizes that patterns repeat, that spiritual principles remain consistent throughout human history.

That's why, when we look at contemporary events through the lens of biblical patterns, we gain extraordinary insight. The battle between Cain and Abel continues in ideological conflicts. The choice between Barabbas and Jesus manifests in our political decisions. The voice of blood—either crying for vengeance or speaking mercy—determines whether societies move toward chaos or peace.

By recognizing these patterns, we become aware of the spiritual dynamics underlying surface events. We develop discernment to see beyond political rhetoric or cultural trends to the spiritual principles at stake. Most importantly, we learn to align ourselves with God's redemptive purposes rather than being unconsciously pulled into rebellion's gravitational field.

Implementation: Using Biblical Patterns to Understand Current Events

1. **Pattern recognition practice:** Select three major news stories from the past week. For each one, ask: "Does this reflect the pattern of Cain and Abel (hatred of faith by works), the choice between Barabbas and Jesus (rebellion versus righteousness), or the blood that cries out (justice versus mercy)?"
2. **Scripture-to-current events mapping:** Create a journal dedicated to matching biblical patterns with contemporary situations. When you notice a pattern playing out in current events, write down the biblical reference, the current situation, and the principle connecting them.
3. **Divine perspective meditation:** For issues that provoke strong emotions in you, take time to view them through the lens of biblical patterns. Ask God

to help you see beyond your initial reactions to the spiritual dynamics at work.

4. **Cyclic history study:** Research historical parallels to current cultural or political movements. How have similar movements in the past reflected biblical patterns? What can these parallels teach us about likely outcomes today?
5. **Blood-voice awareness:** In situations of conflict or injustice, discern whether voices are calling for vengeance (Abel's blood) or reconciliation (Christ's blood). Practice speaking words aligned with Christ's blood—words of mercy, redemption, and restoration—into divisive situations.

Chapter 5: The Matrix of the Modern World

In 1999, a revolutionary film captured the imagination of millions worldwide. "The Matrix," created by the Wachowski siblings (who were raised in a Christian household), presented a profound allegory that transcended mere entertainment. What many viewers may not have realized is that this sci-fi masterpiece offers one of the most powerful visual illustrations of the spiritual condition of humanity and the transformative power of awakening to truth.

In the film, humanity exists in a simulated reality called "the Matrix," controlled by artificially intelligent machines that have enslaved humans as an energy source. Most people are unaware of their captivity, believing the simulation to be reality. A small group of freed humans, led by Morpheus, fights to liberate others and defeat the machines.

The protagonist, Thomas Anderson (known by his hacker alias "Neo"), is contacted by Morpheus, who offers him a choice: take a blue pill and return to his comfortable illusion, or take a red pill and "see how deep the rabbit hole goes." Neo chooses the red pill, is unplugged from the Matrix, and begins a journey toward becoming "The One" who can defeat the system.

While the Wachowskis' spiritual journey has taken various turns since the film's creation, the Christian symbolism in the original Matrix film is unmistakable and offers profound insights into the Barabbas bias and spiritual awakening.

Consider the names and their meanings: Neo means "new life" or "new one." His given name, Thomas Anderson, breaks down to "Thomas" (the doubting disciple) and "Anderson" meaning "son of man" (a title Jesus often used for himself). The very name captures the journey from doubt to faith, from ordinary humanity to divine purpose.

Morpheus, whose name derives from the Greek word for "change" (as in metamorphosis), represents the Holy Spirit—the change agent who guides, teaches, and transforms. Just as the Holy Spirit leads us from our old nature to becoming more Christ-like, Morpheus guides Neo from his illusory existence to his true identity.

Trinity, whose name obviously references the three persons of the Godhead, provides the sacrificial love that ultimately resurrects Neo after his apparent death. This parallels how divine love resurrects us from spiritual death.

The agents who hunt the freed humans, particularly Agent Smith, represent Satan and his forces. They never call Neo by his chosen identity (Neo) but always as "Mr. Anderson," refusing to acknowledge his transformation and true nature. Similarly, Satan continually tries to define us by our old identity rather than who we are in Christ.

In one pivotal scene, Agent Smith tells Neo: "It seems that you've been living two lives. One of these lives has a future, and one of them does not." This perfectly captures the spiritual reality of living either according to the flesh or according to the Spirit—one path leads to life, the other to death.

The red pill/blue pill scene presents perhaps the most powerful metaphor for spiritual awakening. Morpheus offers Neo a choice: "You take the blue pill, the story ends, you wake up in your bed and believe whatever you want to believe. You take the red pill, you stay in Wonderland, and I show you how deep the rabbit hole goes."

This mirrors the choice we all face: remain in comfortable spiritual unconsciousness or embrace the sometimes difficult truth that sets us free. Jesus often presented similar choices: the narrow gate versus the wide gate, building on rock versus sand, serving God versus serving mammon. The red pill represents the awakening that comes through being born again—seeing beyond the matrix of the world system to spiritual reality.

After taking the red pill, Neo undergoes a painful unplugging process. His eyes hurt because, as Morpheus explains, he's never used them before. This parallels the discomfort of spiritual awakening—when we begin to see the world as it truly is, it can be disorienting and painful. Our old assumptions are challenged; our comfortable illusions shattered.

Neo visits the Oracle, whose name means "word" (connecting to Jesus as the Word of God). She tells him cryptically that being "The One" is ultimately his choice—a profound statement about how faith requires our participation and decision. She doesn't force the truth on him but invites him to discover it for himself, just as God invites us to choose faith rather than forcing it upon us.

Neo's journey culminates in a sacrificial death and resurrection. After being killed by Agent Smith, he is restored to life through Trinity's love and faith in him. He returns with new powers—able to see the Matrix for the code it truly is and manipulate it. This parallels how spiritual rebirth transforms our perception of reality and gives us authority over the systems of this world.

In the film's climactic scene, Neo stops bullets with a raised hand and defeats Agent Smith by entering and exploding his body from within—symbolizing how Christ's entry into our lives destroys the power of darkness from the inside out.

What makes "The Matrix" such a powerful illustration of the Barabbas bias is its visualization of the two states of human existence—enslaved unconsciousness versus liberated awareness. Before taking the red pill, Neo (like all humans in the Matrix) unconsciously participates in and perpetuates the very system that enslaves him. He cannot see beyond his programming.

This is exactly how the Barabbas bias functions in unregenerate humanity. We unconsciously choose rebellion, destruction, and death because we can't perceive spiritual reality clearly. We're operating within a system of illusion, unable to recognize the forces influencing our choices.

When Jesus tells Nicodemus, "Very truly I tell you, no one can see the kingdom of God unless they are born again" (John 3:3), he's describing this same concept. Without spiritual rebirth, we're like humans plugged into the Matrix—blind to the kingdom reality operating all around us.

The scriptural command to "awake, O sleeper, and arise from the dead, and Christ will shine on you" (Ephesians 5:14) perfectly captures this call to consciousness. We are spiritual sleepwalkers until Christ awakens us to reality.

This sleep-state explains why masses of people make choices that harm themselves and others. They're not fully conscious of what they're choosing or why. The crowd that shouted "Give us Barabbas!" wasn't making a rational choice—they were responding to spiritual forces they could neither see nor understand.

Today, we witness this unconscious alignment with destruction in many cultural phenomena. Consider how social media can function as a contemporary matrix—a simulated reality where algorithms determine what we see and believe, often manipulating emotions toward rage rather than reason, division rather than unity.

The echo chambers of modern discourse function like the Matrix's feeding tubes—keeping us docile through comfortable narratives that confirm our biases rather than challenging us with truth. We believe we're making independent choices when we're actually responding to programming.

This is why spiritual awakening is often described in terms of sight: scales falling from eyes, veils being removed, blindness healed. When we encounter Christ, we begin to see reality as it truly is—both its beauty and its brokenness. We recognize the matrix of deception that has shaped our perception and can finally make conscious choices aligned with truth.

During the COVID-19 pandemic, I witnessed this matrix effect firsthand. Millions accepted without question narratives that crumbled under scrutiny. Policies that made little logical sense (like allowing crowds in big-box stores while prohibiting church gatherings) were embraced because they came from "authoritative" sources within the matrix.

Those who questioned the prevailing narrative were labeled "conspiracy theorists"—much like those who questioned the Matrix in the film would be considered dangerous or delusional by those still plugged in. Yet as time passed, many of these "conspiracy theories" proved accurate. The difference between a conspiracy theorist and a prophet is often just a matter of months.

This isn't to suggest that every alternative viewpoint is correct, but rather that spiritual awakening requires the courage to question what the system tells us is reality. It demands the humility to admit we might have been operating under illusions and the strength to embrace truth even when it's uncomfortable.

Like Neo, who initially struggles to accept that his entire life has been a simulation, we resist the painful revelation that our perspectives have been shaped by deception. It's easier to take the blue pill—to return to comfortable unconsciousness. But the red pill of spiritual awakening, though initially disorienting, leads to true freedom.

In the film, Morpheus tells Neo: "The Matrix is everywhere. It is all around us. Even now, in this very room. You can see it when you look out your window or when you turn on your television. You can feel it when you go to work... when you go to church... when you pay your taxes. It is the world that has been pulled over your eyes to blind you from the truth."

Similarly, the Barabbas bias is a veil pulled over humanity's spiritual perception. It operates in our politics, our entertainment, our education systems, our economic structures—anywhere the spirit of rebellion can influence human choice.

But just as the red pill freed Neo to see beyond the Matrix, spiritual rebirth through Christ frees us to see beyond this deception. We begin to recognize the patterns of heaven and the patterns of hell. We develop discernment to distinguish between what aligns with God's kingdom and what aligns with rebellion.

This awakening isn't merely intellectual—it's experiential and transformative. Neo didn't just learn about the Matrix; he was unplugged from it. Similarly, spiritual awakening isn't just adopting new beliefs; it's being fundamentally disconnected from the world system and reconnected to divine reality.

In the latter part of the film, Neo begins to manipulate the Matrix itself—bending spoons, stopping bullets, and ultimately defeating Agent Smith. This represents the spiritual authority that comes with awakening. We're no longer passive participants in the world system but active agents of transformation, empowered to overcome forces that once controlled us.

Jesus promised this same authority to his followers: "I have given you authority to trample on snakes and scorpions and to overcome all the power of the enemy; nothing will harm you" (Luke 10:19). When we awaken to our true identity in Christ, we gain authority over the very forces that once enslaved us.

This explains why spiritual awakening is so threatening to systems of control. Awakened individuals can no longer be manipulated through fear, materialistic desires, or tribal identities. They recognize attempts at spiritual manipulation and refuse to participate. Their allegiance lies with a higher reality.

During the 2020 pandemic, churches that awakened to this reality refused to bow to government overreach. Though initially complying with reasonable public health measures, they recognized when restrictions became tools of control rather than public safety measures. Like Neo seeing through the Matrix's code, they could discern the spiritual forces behind seemingly neutral policies.

This awakening comes with a cost. In the film, Morpheus warns Neo that most people are so dependent on the Matrix that they would fight to protect it. Similarly, those who benefit from the current world system often oppose and persecute those who challenge it. Jesus warned his followers: "If the world hates you, keep in mind that it hated me first" (John 15:18).

Yet the reward of awakening far outweighs its cost. Neo discovers capabilities beyond his imagination once freed from the Matrix. Likewise, spiritual awakening releases potential we never knew we had—gifts, callings, and authority that were dormant while we remained unconsciously plugged into the world system.

The Matrix concludes with Neo speaking directly to the machines controlling the system: "I know you're out there. I can feel you now. I know that you're afraid... You're afraid of change. I don't know the future. I didn't come here to tell you how this is going to end. I came here to tell you how it's going to begin... I'm going to show these people what you don't want them to see. I'm going to show them a world without you. A world without rules and controls, without borders or boundaries. A world where anything is possible. Where we go from there is a choice I leave to you."

This declaration echoes the Great Commission—our call to awaken others to spiritual reality. We're not forcing transformation but inviting it, showing people possibilities beyond the limitations of the world system. We're offering the red pill of spiritual awakening, knowing that each person must choose for themselves.

The Matrix's profound impact on popular culture demonstrates how deeply its message resonates with the human spirit. We intuitively sense that there's more to reality than what we can see—that we're living in some kind of simulation or reduced version of true existence. This intuition points to our spiritual nature and our innate longing for awakening.

When we understand the Barabbas bias through the lens of The Matrix, we recognize that choosing Barabbas isn't just a historical anomaly but a symptom of humanity's enslaved consciousness. Only through spiritual awakening—through taking the red pill of rebirth in Christ—can we begin to see clearly and choose rightly.

Implementation: Awakening to the Reality Behind Cultural Illusions

1. **Media fast challenge:** For one week, disconnect from all news and social media. During this time, pray for clarity and read only scripture. Note how your perspective shifts when you're not being influenced by the "Matrix" of modern information systems.

2. **Narrative questioning practice:** Select three widely accepted cultural narratives (about politics, education, healthcare, etc.). For each one, ask: "What evidence supports this? What counterevidence exists? Who benefits from my believing this? What scriptural principles apply here?" Document your findings.
3. **"Red pill" conversations:** Identify someone in your life who seems to be waking up to spiritual reality. Share your journey of awakening and listen to theirs. Discuss how your perceptions of the world have changed since your spiritual rebirth.
4. **Matrix-spotting exercise:** Throughout your day, notice when you're being emotionally manipulated by media, advertising, or social pressure. Name the manipulation technique and consciously reject it, choosing instead to respond from your awakened identity in Christ.
5. **Authority practice:** Identify one area where you've felt powerless against cultural forces (like anxiety about world events, addiction to social media, or fear of others' opinions). Practice exercising your spiritual authority in this area through declaration, prayer, and conscious choice alignment with God's Word.

Chapter 6: The Political Manifestation of the Barabbas Bias

"We shouldn't mix religion and politics." This statement has become almost axiomatic in modern discourse. Churches fear losing tax-exempt status if they speak on political matters. Politicians shy away from faith-based reasoning to avoid accusations of violating the separation of church and state. The general public often treats these as entirely separate spheres that should never intersect.

Yet this artificial separation is not only impossible to maintain in practice—it directly contradicts the biblical understanding of God's authority. The question isn't whether faith and politics should intersect, but how they should relate to one another. Understanding this relationship reveals why the Barabbas bias manifests so powerfully in political systems and how we can respond as believers.

To grasp this relationship, we must first understand a fundamental truth about God's nature. If I were to ask you, "Is God a king or a priest?" what would your answer be?

Many would answer "King," focusing on God's sovereignty, power, and rulership. Others might say "Priest," emphasizing His mediating role and sacrificial love. The truth is that God is both King and Priest.

In the Old Testament, we encounter a mysterious figure named Melchizedek, described as "king of Salem" and "priest of God Most High" (Genesis 14:18). The name Melchizedek means "king of righteousness," and as king of Salem (meaning "peace"), he was also "king of peace." This dual role as both king and priest foreshadowed Christ, who would unite these offices in Himself.

God's authority flows in two parallel streams: kingly and priestly. The kingly aspect governs, administers justice, and establishes order. The priestly aspect mediates, reconciles, and maintains moral conscience. These two aspects are distinct but complementary, designed to work in harmony while keeping each other accountable.

When our Founding Fathers wrote the Constitution with its separation of church and state, they weren't trying to remove faith from public life. Rather, they were reacting against the model they'd seen in England, where King Henry VIII had declared himself head of the Church of England, effectively subjugating the priestly authority to the kingly.

The pilgrims had fled England seeking freedom to worship according to their conscience, not government dictate. The separation they envisioned wasn't to silence the church's moral voice but to prevent the government from controlling religious expression and belief.

The Founders understood that when government controls the church, it silences the prophetic voice that holds power accountable, leading to unchecked corruption. We see this throughout history—even Jerusalem, the holy city, became a "cesspool of corruption" in Jesus' words when the priesthood was overrun by political power.

The healthy relationship between these authorities is separation with interconnection. They should remain distinct yet engaged with one another—the church speaking prophetic truth to power, and the government respecting the moral conscience formed by faith while governing justly.

When this balance is maintained, civilization flourishes. When it's disrupted—when either authority seeks to dominate or silence the other—society deteriorates.

This brings us to the Barabbas bias in politics. Throughout history, we can identify two competing governmental philosophies: those that honor God and those that replace God. The contrast between their fruits couldn't be more stark.

Every government that has attempted to replace God—from Nimrod's Babylon to Pharaoh's Egypt, from Nazi Germany to Stalin's Soviet Union, from Pol Pot's Cambodia to various modern totalitarian regimes—has been guilty of the greatest homicidal and genocidal atrocities. Hundreds of millions have died under regimes that explicitly reject God and make the state the ultimate authority.

Conversely, governments that have embraced Judeo-Christian principles and respected the distinct role of faith have generally fostered human flourishing, prosperity, innovation, and what we might call civilization with civil in it. This isn't to suggest such governments are perfect—they certainly aren't—but the overall pattern is clear.

This pattern brings us back to the Barabbas bias. Recall that Barabbas was guilty of insurrection, rebellion, and murder—the very crimes that caused Lucifer to be cast from heaven. When governments reject God's authority structure, they invariably embody these same characteristics, creating systems that rebel against divine order, foment unrest, and ultimately deal in death rather than life.

We saw this vividly during the COVID-19 pandemic. Many governments seized unprecedented control over citizens' lives—dictating when they could leave their homes, what businesses could operate, and even whether they could gather for worship. What began as temporary emergency measures quickly evolved into lingering power grabs that extended far beyond any public health necessity.

In San Diego, we were told churches couldn't meet because of the virus, yet casinos, strip clubs, Walmart, and Home Depot could operate with minimal restrictions. The message was clear: faith was "non-essential" while commerce and entertainment were "essential." This wasn't about science but about values and priorities.

When I decided to reopen our church against government mandates, we received forty-eight $10,000 fines. We were labeled "conspiracy theorists," "super-spreaders," and "grandma killers"—even by other pastors who chose compliance over conscience. Yet as time passed, virtually every "conspiracy theory" we were accused of promoting has been validated. The social distancing guidelines were arbitrary, mask efficacy was overstated, and treatments like ivermectin (which we helped our congregants obtain from Mexico) proved effective while government-promoted interventions often caused harm.

This wasn't merely about public health but about a manifestation of the Barabbas bias in governance—a preference for control over freedom, for fear over faith, for man's wisdom over God's design. The governments that imposed the most draconian measures were often those most explicitly secular in their orientation.

We see this bias operating in countless other political issues. Consider how our legal system often functions: we provide extensive protections and considerations for the most hardened criminals while simultaneously advocating for the termination of innocent unborn life. This inversion—protecting the guilty while harming the innocent—is the Barabbas bias in action.

When someone who opposes the death penalty for serial killers also supports abortion up to and even after birth (as some politicians now openly advocate), they're exhibiting the same bias the crowd showed when they shouted, "Release Barabbas! Crucify Jesus!"

We witness this in international relations as well. After Islamic extremists commit acts of terrorism, many Western leaders rush to condemn not the ideology that motivated the violence but anyone who might speak critically of that ideology. The victims are quickly forgotten while the narrative shifts to preventing "Islamophobia" rather than addressing the root causes of violence.

This bias operates in the strange attraction many Western intellectuals have felt toward failed communist and socialist systems. Despite communism's consistent record of economic devastation, human rights abuses, and mass casualties, many academic and political elites continue to romanticize collectivist ideologies while denigrating free-market systems that have lifted billions from poverty.

We've seen it in the bizarre hostility directed at political figures who champion traditional values, national sovereignty, and individual liberty. Donald Trump serves as a clear example. Despite policies that benefited minority communities with historically low unemployment, peace initiatives in the Middle East, and criminal justice reform, he faced levels of vitriol and opposition unprecedented in modern politics.

When asked why they hate such figures, many critics cannot articulate specific policy objections beyond emotional reactions: "He's just evil," "He's literally Hitler," "He's destroying democracy." This isn't reasoned political disagreement but spiritual alignment with rebellion against divine order.

Conversely, political figures who embody corruption often receive protection from the same voices. Evidence of serious ethical breaches or self-enrichment schemes gets minimized or dismissed entirely. Media outlets that relentlessly pursue one political side ignore credible allegations against another. This inconsistency isn't merely partisan bias but spiritual alignment with the rebellious nature of Barabbas.

The Biden family laptop controversy illustrates this dynamic perfectly. Despite clear evidence of concerning international business dealings and potential influence peddling, many major media outlets dismissed it as "Russian disinformation" until well after the election, when they quietly acknowledged its authenticity. Compare this to the treatment of Trump, who sacrificed financially during his presidency, leaving office with less wealth than when he entered.

This isn't about partisan politics—similar dynamics exist across the political spectrum and throughout history. The Barabbas bias transcends political affiliations, manifesting wherever human nature remains untransformed by divine grace.

The political manifestation of this bias becomes most dangerous when government attempts to usurp both roles—becoming both king and priest. When the state positions itself as the ultimate moral authority, determining what is true, good, and beautiful without reference to transcendent standards, tyranny inevitably follows.

This is why totalitarian regimes always target religious institutions. They cannot tolerate a competing moral voice. Churches, synagogues, and other houses of worship must either be coopted to serve the state's ideology or silenced. Religious education must be replaced with state indoctrination. Family authority must be subordinated to government authority.

We see this pattern emerging in Western democracies that were once bastions of religious liberty. Christian business owners face legal penalties for operating according to their conscience. Parents lose custody of children for refusing gender transition treatments. Pastors are arrested for preaching biblical views on marriage and sexuality. Religious schools lose accreditation for maintaining faith-based standards of conduct.

These aren't isolated incidents but symptoms of the Barabbas bias operating at a systemic level—the rebellious nature seeking to silence the voice of divine order.

What makes this particularly insidious is that it often operates under noble-sounding banners: "equality," "tolerance," "safety," "public health." Just as Satan disguises himself as an angel of light, the Barabbas bias in governance disguises control as compassion and censorship as protection.

During COVID, government overreach wasn't marketed as "We want to control your lives" but as "We're keeping you safe." The suppression of religious liberty isn't framed as "We're silencing God's voice" but as "We're protecting vulnerable populations from hate." The centralization of power isn't presented as "We're building a totalitarian state" but as "We're ensuring equity and justice."

This deception proves effective because unregenerate human nature has an affinity for rebellion disguised as virtue. Without spiritual discernment, people readily embrace policies and leaders that embody the Barabbas nature while rejecting those aligned with divine principles.

The spiritual nature of this conflict explains why political differences have become so intractable. We're not merely witnessing policy disagreements but spiritual alignments. This is why reasonable arguments often fail to persuade—we're dealing with spiritual bias, not just intellectual positions.

How, then, should believers engage politically in a world dominated by the Barabbas bias? We must begin by recognizing that political involvement isn't optional for Christians—it's an essential aspect of our witness and responsibility.

Jesus commanded us to be "salt and light" in the world. Salt preserves what is good and prevents decay. Light exposes darkness and guides toward truth. These metaphors describe active engagement, not passive withdrawal. When Christians abandon the political sphere, we abandon our responsibility to preserve what is good and illuminate what is true in governmental affairs.

However, our engagement must be distinctively Christ-like rather than merely partisan. We represent a King whose kingdom transcends human political categories. While we may align with certain policies or parties on specific issues, our ultimate allegiance is to God's kingdom, not human political movements.

This means we must be prophetic toward all sides of the political spectrum, speaking truth to power regardless of which party holds that power. Like the Old Testament prophets who confronted kings of their own nation, we must be willing to challenge leaders even when they're "our side" if they depart from biblical principles.

Our engagement should be characterized by both truth and grace—never compromising on fundamental moral principles yet extending compassion to those with whom we disagree. We must avoid the twin errors of harsh judgmentalism lacking love and spineless acceptance lacking conviction.

Most importantly, we must recognize that political change ultimately flows from spiritual transformation. While we advocate for just policies and righteous leadership, we understand that the root problem in politics is the same Barabbas bias that affects all of unregenerate humanity. The ultimate solution isn't a different party or policy but spiritual rebirth that transforms human nature from its rebellious state to alignment with God's order.

This doesn't mean we abandon political action while waiting for spiritual revival. Rather, we pursue both simultaneously—working for just laws and systems while praying for and facilitating spiritual awakening. Political engagement becomes one aspect of our broader mission to see God's kingdom manifest "on earth as it is in heaven."

As we engage politically, we must be wise as serpents yet innocent as doves, recognizing manipulation tactics used to activate the Barabbas bias. These include:

1. **False dilemmas** that present only two extreme options, ignoring balanced approaches
2. **Emotional manipulation** that bypasses reason to trigger knee-jerk reactions
3. **Identity politics** that define people by immutable characteristics rather than character and ideas
4. **Shifting language** that changes definitions of words to advance ideological agendas
5. **Demonization** of opponents that makes reasonable discussion impossible

By recognizing these tactics, we can resist being unconsciously pulled into alignment with rebellion while maintaining constructive engagement.

The story of Joseph in Egypt provides a powerful model for political engagement. Joseph maintained his faith and moral integrity while serving in a pagan government, using his position to preserve life and implement wise policies. He didn't compromise his faith to gain influence, nor did he withdraw from government service because of Egypt's paganism. Instead, he served faithfully where God placed him, becoming an instrument of divine provision during crisis.

Daniel offers a similar example, serving multiple foreign kings without compromising his faith. He respected governmental authority where possible but drew clear lines when asked to violate God's commands. His consistent integrity earned him influence that he used to glorify God and benefit others.

These biblical examples teach us that political engagement isn't about seizing power but about faithful presence and principled influence. We're called to be in the world but not of it—engaged without being corrupted, influential without being compromised.

As we navigate the political manifestation of the Barabbas bias, we must remember that our ultimate hope isn't in human government but in God's kingdom. No election, court decision, or policy change will solve humanity's fundamental problem—our rebellious nature that chooses Barabbas over Jesus. Only spiritual transformation can address this root issue.

Yet this reality doesn't absolve us of political responsibility. Rather, it frames that responsibility within its proper context. We engage politically not as those whose ultimate hope rests in political outcomes but as representatives of a King whose government will have no end.

By understanding the Barabbas bias in politics, we can engage more effectively, avoid unconscious alignment with rebellion, and maintain our distinct identity as citizens of heaven while being responsibly involved citizens on earth.

Implementation: Engaging Politically Without Falling Prey to Spiritual Manipulation

1. **Biblical policy evaluation:** Before adopting a political position, examine it against scripture rather than party platforms. List three key issues and identify relevant biblical principles that should shape your view.
2. **Media diversification:** Intentionally consume news from sources across the political spectrum,

comparing how different outlets cover the same events. Notice manipulation tactics and practice discerning fact from spin.

3. **Principled prayer practice:** Commit to praying regularly for leaders you disagree with politically. Ask God to bless them and guide them toward truth and righteousness, not just toward your preferred policies.
4. **Kingdom perspective check:** When political events provoke strong emotions, pause and ask: "How important will this be in light of eternity? What kingdom principles transcend this temporary situation?" Record your reflections.
5. **Responsible citizenship audit:** Evaluate your political engagement across five dimensions: prayer for leaders, knowledge of issues, community involvement, voting, and civil discourse. Identify where you need growth and create a specific plan for improvement.

Chapter 7: From Youth Pastor to Culture Warrior

I never planned to become what some might call a "culture warrior." My journey began with a simple desire to work with young people, to make Christianity relevant and exciting for a generation that often found church boring and disconnected from their lives. Yet God has a way of taking our plans and reshaping them into His purpose—sometimes leading us to places we never anticipated.

For fifteen years, my wife and I poured our hearts into youth ministry. The first seven years were in New Zealand, followed by another seven years at a thriving church on Sydney's Northern beaches in Australia. Youth ministry suited my personality perfectly—I often describe it as the "Peter Pan of ministry" because you never have to grow up. You get to be edgy, push boundaries, and have a street credibility that senior pastors rarely enjoy.

Our approach to youth ministry was anything but conventional. We created a character called "Pulse Man," named after our youth group, P.U.L.S.E. He wore a Superman outfit with the "S" changed to a "P" and a John Travolta mask. The teenager who played Pulse Man wanted to be a stuntman, so we'd film him performing increasingly outrageous stunts.

In one memorable incident, he filled a mall fountain with detergent until it overflowed with bubbles, then dove in wearing goggles and flippers. Security guards arrested him while our hidden cameras captured everything. Another time, he attempted to ride his BMX bike off a cliff into a blowhole during high surf. He hit a rock and nearly lost his life, emerging from the water still clutching his handlebars.

After each stunt, we'd play our jingle: "Yeah, he's Pulse Man! He can do anything you can't! He's Pulse Man!" The following Friday, 250 students would show up, with Pulse Man signing autographs like a celebrity.

We "borrowed" shopping carts from local grocery stores, found the steepest hill in town, put kids in flimsy plastic helmets, and pushed them down. They'd crash into curbs and parked cars, sometimes sustaining minor injuries, but everyone thought we were the coolest youth leaders around.

Behind these antics was serious purpose. We combined these attention-grabbing stunts with powerful worship, biblical teaching, and genuine discipleship. We saw hundreds of teenagers encounter Christ, many of whom are now in ministry themselves. We grew from 50 kids to over 1,000, active in high schools across the region.

I loved being what I call "a little bit edgy, a little bit naughty." As the youth pastor, I could push boundaries; that was my job. Senior pastors define boundaries—they're the responsible adults in the room. So when my senior pastor in Sydney sat down with me after seven years and asked, "Have you ever thought that there might be a church in you?" I was conflicted.

Yes, I had considered it, but I was reluctant to leave the fun and freedom of youth ministry. I enjoyed the creativity, the energy, and even the craziness of working with teenagers. Being a senior pastor seemed so... serious.

Yet something in me resonated with his question. There was a church in me—a vision for a community of believers that would impact not just youth but entire families and cities. After prayer and reflection, my wife and I felt God calling us to San Diego to plant what would become Awaken Church.

In 2005, we arrived in Southern California with a vision of one church in four locations. Within 19 years, God expanded that vision beyond anything we could have imagined. Today, Awaken Church has grown to ten locations across four states—California, Idaho, Utah, and Washington—with plans to expand into Florida.

The transition from youth pastor to senior pastor required significant personal growth. I had to develop new leadership skills, mature in my approach to ministry, and learn to carry the weight of responsibility for an entire congregation rather than just one demographic. Yet I never lost that creative edge and willingness to challenge conventions that had made our youth ministry successful.

By 2020, Awaken Church had grown to about 5,000 members across five campuses. We were seeing lives transformed, communities impacted, and the kingdom of God expanding through our ministry. Then came what I consider a pivotal testing period—a moment that would transform me from pastor to culture warrior.

The year 2020 itself is significant numerically—adding up to 40, which in the Bible consistently represents testing.

Moses was tested in the wilderness for 40 years, Jesus was tested by the devil for 40 days, the children of Israel wandered for 40 years. Additionally, ophthalmologists tell us that "20/20" represents ideal vision, but perfect 20/20 vision doesn't really exist—except in hindsight. This seemed prophetic, suggesting that what we would experience in 2020 wouldn't make sense until we looked back at it.

When COVID-19 hit, like most churches, we initially complied with lockdown orders. For about six weeks, we observed social distancing, mask mandates, and capacity restrictions. We pivoted to online services and found ways to minister within the constraints placed upon us.

But as weeks passed, something within me began to rebel against what I perceived as government overreach. This reaction wasn't just political—it was visceral, almost like an allergic response. I believe it was connected to my family history.

My father had grown up in East Germany under communist rule. He experienced firsthand the oppressive nature of totalitarian government—the restricted movement, the surveillance, the punishment for dissent. He spent 26 months in a concentration camp for refusing to shoot a defector and for commenting that West German uniforms looked superior to East German ones. When released, he risked his life crossing a minefield to escape to freedom.

Recent scientific studies have shown that trauma can be imprinted on DNA. Researchers can determine with remarkable accuracy whether someone had relatives who experienced the Holocaust through DNA testing. The trauma doesn't just affect the individual but can be passed down genetically to future generations.

I believe my reaction to government overreach during COVID was connected to this inherited trauma. When I saw arbitrary restrictions being placed on religious gatherings while businesses like Walmart and Home Depot operated freely, something in me recognized the familiar pattern of government using a crisis to control religious expression.

The inconsistencies were glaring. We were told churches couldn't meet because of virus transmission risks, but casinos and strip clubs could operate. We were instructed that singing in church was dangerous, but shouting at protests was perfectly safe. Science wasn't driving these distinctions—values and priorities were.

After much prayer and consideration, I made the difficult decision to reopen our church against government mandates. This wasn't done lightly or rebelliously, but out of conviction that we had a constitutional right and spiritual obligation to gather for worship.

The response was swift and severe. We received forty-eight $10,000 fines. We made front-page news as media outlets portrayed us as reckless and dangerous. We were labeled "conspiracy theorists," "super-spreaders," and "grandma killers"—even by fellow pastors who chose compliance over conscience.

What surprised me most was the division within the body of Christ. Pastors I had considered friends distanced themselves from us. Some publicly criticized our stance. The church seemed as polarized as the wider culture, with COVID response becoming a litmus test for where one stood politically and theologically.

Despite the criticism, we stood firm. We implemented common-sense precautions while refusing to close our doors. Our conviction was that the church is essential—perhaps more essential during times of crisis than ever before. People needed hope, community, and spiritual guidance as they navigated unprecedented challenges.

What happened next was remarkable. While many churches struggled to regain pre-pandemic attendance when they finally reopened, our church doubled in size. By the end of 2021, we had grown from 5,000 to 10,000 members. People drove from hours away to attend a church that was open when their local churches remained closed.

This growth wasn't just about being open when others weren't. It reflected a hunger for spiritual leadership that wouldn't bow to cultural and governmental pressure—that would stand firm on conviction even when it was costly to do so.

As time passed, many of our positions were validated. Social distancing guidelines proved arbitrary, mask efficacy was overstated, and treatments like ivermectin (which we helped our congregants obtain from Mexico) proved effective while government-promoted interventions like Remdesivir showed serious side effects—so serious that many medical professionals quietly called it "Run-Death-Is-Near."

Despite thousands in our church contracting COVID, we had zero deaths—largely because we educated our members about early treatment options and prevented them from receiving harmful protocols. We weren't just standing for religious freedom but for truth in a time of widespread misinformation.

This stance against prevailing narratives transformed me from pastor to culture warrior. I found myself speaking out not just on spiritual matters but on issues of medical freedom, government overreach, and media manipulation. Interviews and speaking invitations came from secular sources interested in our countercultural stance.

This wasn't a role I sought, but one I embraced as necessary for the moment. Throughout scripture, we see that spiritual leaders often play different roles in different seasons. Nathan was David's spiritual advisor but became his prophetic confronter when the king strayed into sin. Joseph was a dreamer who became a political leader during crisis. Esther was a beauty queen who became an advocate for her people facing extinction.

The times determine the role God calls us to play. In seasons of peace and prosperity, pastors may focus primarily on spiritual formation and community building. In seasons of cultural crisis and moral decline, we may be called to a more prophetic, confrontational role.

This shift wasn't without cost. The criticism intensified. Relationships strained. Our church became polarizing—people either strongly supported our stance or strongly opposed it. The comfortable middle ground disappeared.

Yet with this cost came unexpected blessings. People hungry for truth and courage found a spiritual home at Awaken. Believers who felt isolated in their convictions discovered community. Those disillusioned with institutional Christianity that seemed more concerned with cultural approval than biblical fidelity found renewed faith.

Our growth during this period wasn't just numerical but spiritual. Crisis has a way of separating the sincere from the superficial, the committed from the casual. Those who remained and those who joined during this time were believers willing to count the cost of their faith—to stand firm even when it wasn't popular or convenient.

This experience deepened my understanding of the Barabbas bias. I witnessed firsthand how masses could be manipulated into supporting restrictions on fundamental freedoms in the name of safety. I saw how quickly people abandoned constitutional principles when fear dominated the narrative. I observed the hostility directed at those who questioned official narratives, even when those questions were reasonable and evidence-based.

The COVID crisis revealed that the spiritual forces behind the Barabbas bias—the preference for control over freedom, fear over faith, man's wisdom over God's design—operate not just in ancient history but in our contemporary context. The crowd that shouted "Give us Barabbas!" has modern counterparts shouting "Close the churches!" "Mandate the vaccines!" "Silence the dissenters!"

This realization transformed how I understand pastoral leadership in the modern age. Being a faithful shepherd today requires more than preaching good sermons and providing pastoral care. It demands cultural discernment, courageous advocacy, and a willingness to stand against prevailing winds when they blow contrary to biblical truth.

This doesn't mean adopting a permanently combative posture or seeing enemies everywhere. Culture war for its own sake is spiritually destructive. Rather, it means recognizing when cultural forces threaten fundamental truths and freedoms, and being willing to stand firm in those moments, regardless of cost.

Jesus himself modeled this balanced approach. He wasn't constantly confrontational, but he didn't shrink from necessary conflicts. He called out religious hypocrisy, challenged unjust systems, and refused to bow to cultural expectations that contradicted his mission. Yet he also knew when to withdraw from conflict, when to speak gently rather than forcefully, when to build bridges rather than draw battle lines.

The challenge for pastors today is discerning which issues demand a warrior stance and which allow for a more conciliatory approach. Not every cultural disagreement warrants the same level of resistance. We must distinguish between preferences that can accommodate diversity and principles that require firm stands.

For me, religious freedom is non-negotiable. The right to gather for worship, to preach the full counsel of God, to operate according to biblical convictions—these are principles worth fighting for. When government oversteps its bounds to restrict these fundamental freedoms, resistance becomes not just permissible but necessary.

This stance isn't about partisan politics but biblical principles. Throughout history, overreaching government power has come from both left and right. The issue isn't which party holds power but whether that power respects God-given boundaries.

As Awaken Church continues to grow across multiple states, I'm more convinced than ever that the church must be both prophetic and pastoral, both culturally engaged and spiritually focused. We cannot retreat into a religious bubble while the culture crumbles around us, nor can we become so focused on cultural battles that we neglect our primary mission of making disciples.

The journey from youth pastor to senior pastor to culture warrior has taught me that leadership evolves with the times. The edgy creativity that made our youth ministry effective hasn't disappeared but has found new expression in courageous cultural engagement. The willingness to push boundaries that once manifested in Pulse Man stunts now manifests in standing against governmental overreach.

Through it all, the mission remains the same: to see people encounter Christ, communities transformed, and God's kingdom advance. The methods may change with the seasons, but the message of redemption, restoration, and renewal remains constant.

For pastors and believers navigating similar waters, I offer this encouragement: Be willing to evolve in your leadership. Don't be afraid to take stands when conviction demands it. Recognize that faithfulness sometimes requires confrontation, even when that brings criticism and cost. And remember that the same God who called you to ministry will sustain you when that ministry becomes challenging and controversial.

The path from youth pastor to culture warrior wasn't one I planned, but it's one I've embraced as necessary for such a time as this. Whatever path God has you on, may you have the courage to follow it faithfully, even when it leads to unexpected and challenging places.

Implementation: Leading Courageously When Conviction Demands It

1. **Conviction clarity exercise:** List your non-negotiable convictions—principles you would stand for regardless of opposition or cost. For each, identify the biblical basis and why this principle is essential rather than preferential.
2. **Cost calculation practice:** Before taking a controversial stand, prayerfully consider both the cost of speaking up and the cost of staying silent. Journal about potential consequences of both choices, asking God for wisdom to discern when courage requires voice and when it requires restraint.
3. **Courageous conversation preparation:** Identify a truth you believe needs to be spoken in your sphere of influence. Practice articulating this truth

with both courage and compassion, anticipating objections and preparing gracious responses.

4. **Support network development:** Create a list of 3-5 trusted advisors who will both encourage your courageous stands and honestly challenge you when your approach needs adjustment. Meet with them regularly for accountability and perspective.
5. **Criticism resilience building:** Develop a healthy process for handling criticism. This might include: distinguishing between constructive and destructive criticism, having designated times to review feedback rather than constant monitoring, identifying truth in even harsh criticism, and practicing self-care during periods of intense opposition.

Chapter 8: Responding to Tyranny: Lessons from 2020

The year 2020 marked a defining moment for churches and spiritual leaders across America and around the world. What began as "fifteen days to flatten the curve" evolved into months of restrictions, mandates, and unprecedented government involvement in religious gatherings. How we responded to this crisis revealed much about our understanding of scripture, our view of government authority, and our courage to stand on conviction when it comes at a cost.

The numeric symbolism of 2020 itself is striking. In scripture, the number 40 (20+20=40) consistently represents testing. Moses was tested in the wilderness for 40 years. Jesus was tested by Satan for 40 days. The children of Israel wandered 40 years in the desert. Noah endured the flood for 40 days and 40 nights. Whenever you see the number 40 in scripture, you can be certain testing is taking place.

Additionally, ophthalmologists use 20/20 to represent ideal vision. Yet perfect vision doesn't truly exist in the present—it's only available in hindsight. This suggests that the events of 2020 would only make sense as we looked back and gained perspective on what we experienced.

The testing nature of 2020 became evident as churches faced an unprecedented dilemma: comply with government restrictions on gatherings or stand firm on the biblical mandate to assemble. This wasn't merely a practical decision but a theological one that forced us to examine biblical principles regarding government authority, religious liberty, and the essential nature of corporate worship.

When COVID-19 first emerged, like most churches, Awaken Church initially complied with shutdown orders. For approximately six weeks, we observed social distancing, mask requirements, and capacity restrictions. We pivoted to online services and found creative ways to minister within these constraints.

However, as weeks passed, the restrictions began to show concerning patterns that went beyond public health concerns. Churches faced stricter limitations than businesses deemed "essential." Walmart, Home Depot, liquor stores, and even strip clubs could operate with modifications, while churches were completely prohibited from gathering in many jurisdictions.

The inconsistencies were glaring. We were told singing in church was dangerous due to respiratory droplets, yet shouting at political protests was actively encouraged by many of the same officials restricting worship. Science wasn't driving these distinctions—values and priorities were.

As I observed these inconsistencies, something within me began to rebel against what I perceived as government overreach. This reaction wasn't just political—it was visceral, almost like an allergic response. I believe it was connected to my family history and what scientists now recognize as generational trauma passed through DNA.

My father grew up in East Germany under communist rule. He witnessed firsthand how totalitarian governments use crises to expand control, restrict freedoms, and particularly target religious expression. He spent 26 months in a concentration camp for refusing to shoot a defector and for comments deemed disloyal to the regime. When released, he risked his life crossing a minefield to escape to freedom.

Recent scientific research has demonstrated that trauma can be imprinted on DNA and passed to subsequent generations. Studies can determine with remarkable accuracy whether someone had relatives who experienced the Holocaust through DNA testing alone. The body's adaptations to extreme conditions become encoded genetically and influence later generations.

I believe my instinctive reaction against government restrictions during COVID was connected to this inherited trauma. Something in my spiritual and perhaps even genetic makeup recognized the familiar pattern of government using emergency powers to control religious expression, often with no defined end point.

After much prayer and consideration, I made the difficult decision to reopen our church against government mandates. This wasn't done lightly or rebelliously but out of conviction that we had both a constitutional right and spiritual obligation to gather for worship.

The response was swift and severe. We accumulated forty-eight $10,000 fines—nearly half a million dollars in penalties that we refused to pay. Media outlets portrayed us as reckless and dangerous. We were labeled "conspiracy theorists," "super-spreaders," and "grandma killers"—even by fellow pastors who chose compliance over conscience.

The division within the body of Christ was perhaps the most painful aspect of this experience. Pastors I had considered friends publicly criticized our stance. Churches that had previously partnered with us distanced themselves. The church seemed as polarized as the wider culture, with COVID response becoming a litmus test for where one stood not just politically but theologically.

Yet amid this opposition, something remarkable happened. While many churches struggled to regain pre-pandemic attendance when they finally reopened, our church doubled in size. By the end of 2021, we had grown from 5,000 to 10,000 members. People drove from hours away to attend a church that was open when their local churches remained closed.

This growth wasn't merely because we were open when others weren't. It reflected a hunger for spiritual leadership that wouldn't bow to cultural and governmental pressure—that would stand firm on conviction even when it was costly to do so.

As time passed, many of our positions were validated. The social distancing guidelines proved arbitrary and inconsistently applied. Mask efficacy was significantly overstated, particularly for cloth masks most commonly used. Treatments like ivermectin and hydroxychloroquine (which we helped our congregants obtain from Mexico) showed effectiveness while being actively suppressed in public discourse.

Perhaps most importantly, despite thousands in our church contracting COVID, we experienced zero deaths. This wasn't merely good fortune but the result of educating our members about early treatment options and preventing them from receiving harmful protocols like Remdesivir and ventilator treatment that many medical professionals quietly referred to as "Run-Death-Is-Near."

Our experience during 2020 raises profound questions about how Christians should respond to government mandates that restrict religious freedom. Scripture provides guidance that's more nuanced than either blind compliance or reflexive rebellion.

Romans 13 instructs believers to submit to governing authorities, recognizing that God has established governmental authority for maintaining order and punishing wrongdoing. This passage has often been cited to advocate complete compliance with government directives.

However, scripture also shows us that submission to government is not absolute. When government commands what God forbids or forbids what God commands, believers must "obey God rather than men" (Acts 5:29). Daniel continued praying despite the king's decree against it. The Hebrew midwives disobeyed Pharaoh's order to kill Hebrew boys. The early apostles continued preaching despite being ordered to stop.

The key question becomes: Was gathering for worship during a pandemic something God commands that government was forbidding? I believe the answer is yes. Hebrews 10:25 explicitly instructs believers not to neglect meeting together, and this gathering is presented not as optional but essential to the Christian life. Throughout scripture and church history, the assembly of believers has been central to Christian practice.

While temporary adjustments during genuine emergencies may be appropriate, indefinite suspension of gatherings crosses into the territory of forbidding what God commands. This is particularly true when the restrictions appear motivated by values and priorities that place religious exercise in a "non-essential" category while protecting commercial and political activities.

Beyond biblical principles, the American context adds constitutional considerations. The First Amendment specifically protects religious exercise from government interference. While courts have recognized limited exceptions for compelling government interests, these must be narrowly tailored and applied equally to comparable activities.

The disparate treatment of religious gatherings compared to commercial and political gatherings during COVID violated this principle of equal application. Churches were subjected to stricter standards than businesses and protests, revealing that something beyond public health was driving these distinctions.

Our experience during 2020 provided several crucial lessons about responding to government overreach:

First, courage is contagious. When we took our stand, numerous other churches found the courage to reopen as well. Many pastors privately expressed support while feeling unable to take the same stand in their contexts. Our willingness to face consequences created space for others to exercise their religious freedom.

Second, convictions come with costs. The fines, negative publicity, and broken relationships were real prices we paid for our stance. Courage isn't the absence of consequences but the willingness to face them for something more important than comfort or approval.

Third, discernment requires looking beyond stated rationales to underlying motivations. Throughout the pandemic, many policies were presented as "following the science" when they actually reflected values, priorities, and often, political considerations. Spiritual discernment means examining not just what is being required but why and to what end.

Fourth, dissent is sometimes the most faithful position. While scripture generally encourages respect for authority, it never endorses blind compliance that violates conscience or biblical commands. There are times when faithful Christian witness requires standing against prevailing winds, even when they blow from governing authorities.

Fifth, division is inevitable when convictions clash. Jesus himself said he came not to bring peace but a sword (Matthew 10:34)—not because he valued division but because truth sometimes necessitates separation from those unwilling to stand for it. While we should pursue unity where possible, we must recognize that unity purchased at the price of conviction is too expensive.

The COVID crisis also revealed the power of fear to override both reason and principle. Many who normally championed constitutional freedoms readily abandoned them when presented with sufficiently frightening scenarios. Churches that normally emphasized the lordship of Christ quickly submitted to government restrictions with minimal theological reflection.

Fear has always been one of tyranny's most effective tools. When people are afraid, they willingly surrender freedoms they would otherwise defend. This is why scripture repeatedly commands us not to fear—not because danger isn't real, but because fear impairs discernment and compromises conviction.

Throughout 2020, I observed a direct correlation between fear levels and compliance with questionable mandates. Those most consumed by fear of the virus were most willing to accept any restriction presented as providing safety, regardless of its actual effectiveness or its impact on fundamental freedoms.

This dynamic revealed another aspect of the Barabbas bias—the tendency to choose apparent safety over actual liberty, to prefer controlling systems over personal responsibility. The crowd that chose Barabbas over Jesus wasn't making a reasoned choice but responding emotionally to manipulation by religious and political leaders who stirred their fears and prejudices.

Similarly, the compliance with unprecedented restrictions on religious freedom during COVID wasn't primarily based on careful analysis of data or constitutional principles but on fear amplified by media and government narratives.

This observation isn't meant to dismiss genuine health concerns or suggest the virus wasn't serious. COVID-19 was and is a significant public health challenge that has caused real suffering and loss. However, the response to it revealed how readily fundamental principles can be abandoned when fear dominates the conversation.

For church leaders navigating similar challenges in the future—whether another pandemic, natural disaster, or government action—I offer these practical guidelines:

First, distinguish between temporary accommodations and permanent compromises. Brief adjustments during genuine emergencies differ from indefinite suspensions of biblical mandates. Be clear about time frames and exit strategies when making concessions.

Second, evaluate restrictions based on consistency. If religious activities face stricter limitations than comparable secular activities, this suggests motivations beyond public health concerns. True safety measures should apply equally to similar risk scenarios regardless of their nature.

Third, consider practical alternatives before outright defiance. During our stance against restrictions, we implemented reasonable precautions—offering outdoor options, providing masks for those who wanted them, arranging seating to allow distancing for vulnerable populations—while maintaining our fundamental commitment to gathering.

Fourth, build consensus through education. Before taking our stand, we equipped our congregation with information, biblical principles, and reasoning behind our decisions. This created unity and prepared them for the opposition we would face together.

Fifth, prepare for consequences before taking controversial stands. We anticipated the fines, media attacks, and criticism before reopening. This preparation enabled us to respond thoughtfully rather than reactively when these consequences materialized.

Finally, remember that different contexts may require different applications of the same principles. Our approach in California might not have been appropriate in every location. Local laws, cultural factors, and specific church circumstances should inform how universal principles are applied in particular situations.

As we emerge from the COVID era and reflect on its lessons, it's worth considering how the spiritual discernment required during the pandemic applies to other areas where government intersects with religious practice and belief.

We face increasing pressure to conform to cultural mandates regarding sexuality, gender, and other moral issues. Schools introduce curriculum that contradicts biblical teachings. Medical ethics increasingly diverge from Christian understanding of life's sanctity. Employment and business regulations sometimes require actions that violate religious conscience.

The principles that guided our COVID response apply to these challenges as well. We must distinguish between areas where government has legitimate authority and areas where it oversteps into God's domain. We must be willing to face consequences for conviction while pursuing practical alternatives where possible. We must educate and build consensus rather than merely declaring positions.

Most importantly, we must recognize that spiritual discernment isn't a one-time event but an ongoing process. The specific challenges change, but the need to discern when to submit and when to stand remains constant.

The testing of 2020 revealed much about our priorities, convictions, and courage. Some discovered they valued safety and approval more than they realized. Others found courage they didn't know they possessed. Many churches discovered how quickly fundamental practices could be surrendered when presented with sufficient fear.

If we learn nothing else from this period, let it be this: preparation for challenging times happens before those times arrive. Churches that had already developed clear biblical understanding of government authority, religious liberty, and essential Christian practices weathered the COVID storm with greater clarity and conviction than those trying to formulate theology during crisis.

As we face future challenges—and they will surely come—may we be a people who have done the theological work in advance, who know where our lines of conviction lie, and who have the courage to stand firm when those lines are crossed, regardless of the cost.

Implementation: Discerning When to Submit and When to Stand

1. **Authority boundary mapping:** Create a diagram with three concentric circles representing areas where: (1) government has clear biblical authority; (2) authority is shared between church and state with potential tensions; (3) government has no legitimate biblical authority. Place specific issues in their appropriate circles to clarify your understanding of proper jurisdiction.
2. **Conviction cost assessment:** For each of your core convictions, honestly assess: "What am I willing to lose for this belief?" Consider reputation, relationships, financial security, and legal standing. This clarity helps prepare you for potential challenges before they arise.
3. **Fear identification exercise:** When facing pressure to comply with questionable mandates, list your specific fears about non-compliance. Examine each fear in light of scripture, asking whether your decision is being driven more by these fears than by biblical principles.

4. **Practical alternatives brainstorming:** Before choosing outright defiance of problematic requirements, gather trusted advisors to identify creative alternatives that might satisfy both legal obligations and biblical convictions. Document these options for reference during future challenges.
5. **Emergency preparation planning:** Develop clear guidelines now for how your family, church, or organization will evaluate and respond to government directives during future emergencies. Include biblical principles, decision-making processes, and communication strategies.

Chapter 9: The War Against Truth

In the beginning of time, as recorded in Genesis 1, we find a powerful pattern that reveals one of the most important spiritual principles in scripture. "The earth was formless and void, and darkness covered the face of the deep" (Genesis 1:2). This description—formless, void, and dark—establishes the natural state of things before divine intervention.

The Hebrew words translated as "formless and void" are tohu va bohu, which literally mean "chaos and disorder." So before God's word came, the earth existed in a state of chaos, disorder, and darkness. This wasn't merely a physical description but a spiritual principle that extends throughout history.

Then God spoke: "Let there be light." With these four simple words, divine order began to overcome chaos. The subsequent creative commands—"Let there be a firmament," "Let the waters be gathered," "Let the earth bring forth"—progressively transformed primordial chaos into structured beauty.

This pattern reveals a profound truth: God's word brings order from chaos, light from darkness, and beauty from formlessness. Wherever the word of God is present and honored, order, light, and beauty flourish. Conversely, wherever God's word is removed or rejected, the natural drift is back toward chaos, darkness, and disorder.

Satan understands this principle perfectly. As the "father of lies" (John 8:44), he knows that truth is his greatest enemy. His primary strategy has always been to question, distort, or silence God's word. From his first recorded words in scripture—"Did God really say...?"—to his modern tactics of censorship and distortion, Satan's war against truth remains consistent.

We see this war intensifying in our current cultural moment. There's an unprecedented effort to remove God's word from public schools, government institutions, and cultural discourse. Prayer has been banned from classrooms, the Ten Commandments removed from courthouses, and biblical values increasingly marginalized as "hateful" or "outdated."

This isn't merely a political or cultural shift but a spiritual strategy with predictable consequences. As the word of God has been systematically removed from education, government, entertainment, and even many churches, we've witnessed a corresponding increase in chaos, confusion, and darkness.

Consider what happens in neighborhoods where biblical values are no longer taught and embraced. Crime increases. Family structures collapse. Substance abuse flourishes. Mental health deteriorates. This isn't coincidental but causal—the absence of God's word creates a vacuum where chaos naturally thrives.

We see this pattern throughout Israel's history. When they honored God's law, they prospered and flourished. When they abandoned it for pagan practices, society deteriorated into chaos and eventually judgment. This cycle repeats consistently: adherence to God's word brings blessing; rejection brings cursing—not because God is vindictive but because these are the natural consequences of either aligning with or rejecting divine order.

The Barabbas bias manifests powerfully in this war against truth. Unregenerate human nature has an inherent preference for darkness over light, for chaos over order, for rebellion over submission to divine authority. Jesus described this reality: "Light has come into the world, but people loved darkness instead of light because their deeds were evil" (John 3:19).

This explains why efforts to remove God's word from society often receive surprising popular support. The crowd that chose Barabbas over Jesus is spiritually aligned with those who prefer humanistic philosophies over biblical truth, moral relativism over divine commands, and subjective feelings over objective reality.

The current "post-truth" era, where objective facts matter less than emotional appeals and personal preferences, represents the culmination of this bias. When Oxford Dictionaries declared "post-truth" their Word of the Year in 2016, they defined it as circumstances where "objective facts are less influential in shaping public opinion than appeals to emotion and personal belief." This isn't a new phenomenon but the ancient Barabbas bias in modern form.

What makes this particularly dangerous is the technological amplification available today. Social media algorithms reward emotional content over factual accuracy, creating echo chambers where lies can flourish unchallenged. Mass media outlets increasingly abandon journalistic standards for narrative-driven reporting. Educational institutions teach students to prioritize subjective experience over objective truth.

During COVID-19, we witnessed this war against truth in unprecedented ways. Scientific inquiry, which requires open debate and rigorous questioning, was replaced with appeals to "trust the science"—a phrase that actually contradicts the scientific method. Alternative perspectives from credentialed experts were systematically censored from social media platforms. Data that contradicted official narratives was labeled "misinformation" regardless of its accuracy.

The suppression of treatments like ivermectin and hydroxychloroquine—medications with decades of safety data and significant clinical success against COVID—exemplified this pattern. Rather than following evidence, many institutions followed narratives, with devastating consequences for patients who might have benefited from these treatments.

This wasn't merely political polarization but spiritual warfare against truth itself. The forces that chose Barabbas over Jesus two thousand years ago are the same forces working today to silence voices that speak uncomfortable truths, censor information that challenges preferred narratives, and punish those who refuse to bow to culturally approved falsehoods.

As believers committed to truth, how do we respond effectively to this warfare?

First, we must recognize the supernatural nature of this conflict. Paul reminds us that "our struggle is not against flesh and blood, but against the rulers, against the authorities, against the powers of this dark world and against the spiritual forces of evil in the heavenly realms" (Ephesians 6:12). The war against truth isn't merely cultural or political but spiritual at its core.

This recognition prevents us from demonizing people while confronting destructive ideas. Those promoting falsehoods are often themselves victims of deception rather than conscious agents of darkness. Jesus's prayer from the cross—"Father, forgive them, for they do not know what they are doing" (Luke 23:34)—applies to many caught in Satan's web of lies today.

Second, we must commit to being people of truth in every aspect of life. This begins with personal integrity—refusing to participate in the small deceptions that have become culturally acceptable, from tax evasion to resume embellishment to social media personas that bear little resemblance to reality.

Truth is a seamless garment. We cannot effectively stand for biblical truth in public while practicing deception in private. As Jesus warned the Pharisees, we must clean the inside of the cup first, then the outside will also be clean (Matthew 23:26).

Third, we must saturate ourselves in God's word. If the absence of God's word leads to chaos and darkness, its presence brings order and light. Daily immersion in scripture inoculates us against the prevalent lies of our culture and gives us discernment to recognize truth from counterfeit.

Psalm 119:105 declares, "Your word is a lamp for my feet, a light on my path." In a darkening cultural landscape, scripture provides illumination that enables us to navigate complex issues with divine wisdom rather than human opinion.

Fourth, we must speak truth with both courage and compassion. Truth without love becomes a weapon; love without truth becomes sentimentality. Ephesians 4:15 instructs us to "speak the truth in love," maintaining both elements in proper balance.

This requires discernment about when to speak boldly and when to speak gently, when public confrontation is necessary and when private conversation is more appropriate. Jesus himself demonstrated different approaches in different contexts—sometimes speaking with gentle compassion to individuals, other times publicly confronting systems and leaders who misled others.

Fifth, we must create and support alternative systems and institutions committed to truth. As mainstream educational institutions, media outlets, and cultural producers increasingly abandon commitment to objective truth, we must build alternatives that honor God's word and pursue truth wherever it leads.

This might include starting or supporting Christian schools, creating media outlets committed to factual reporting, developing technology platforms that don't censor biblical perspectives, and building businesses that operate with integrity and excellence.

Sixth, we must recognize and reject manipulation tactics used in the war against truth. These include:

- **Emotionalism** that elevates feelings over facts

- **Euphemistic language** that disguises evil with pleasant-sounding terms
- **False consensus** that portrays deviant positions as mainstream
- **Assertion of inevitability** that presents harmful changes as unstoppable
- **Redefinition of terms** to subvert traditional meanings
- **Appeal to "progress"** that assumes moral evolution rather than decline
- **Demonization of dissenters** that attacks people rather than addressing their arguments

Finally, we must maintain hope in truth's ultimate triumph. Jesus declared, "I am the way, the truth, and the life" (John 14:6)—identifying himself with truth itself. When we stand for truth, we stand with Christ, who has already overcome the world and its deceptions.

The war against truth is not new, nor is its outcome uncertain. Throughout history, God has preserved a remnant committed to his word even during the darkest periods. Light always eventually exposes darkness; truth ultimately prevails over falsehood. Our role is to remain faithful guardians of truth in our generation, trusting God with the final results.

During my experience standing against COVID restrictions, I witnessed both the intensity of the war against truth and the power of truth to eventually prevail. Information we were banned from sharing in 2020 became acknowledged facts by 2022. Perspectives labeled "dangerous misinformation" were later validated by peer-reviewed studies. Truth suppressed eventually resurfaces, often with greater impact than if it had been permitted free expression initially.

This pattern should encourage us to stand firm even when truth seems overwhelmed by falsehood. As Martin Luther King Jr. famously observed, "The arc of the moral universe is long, but it bends toward justice." Similarly, while the war against truth may seem to be advancing in certain moments, the ultimate trajectory of history bends toward truth's triumph.

The Barabbas bias inclines unregenerate humanity to prefer comforting lies over uncomfortable truths, but this preference cannot permanently suppress reality. Facts, as John Adams noted, "are stubborn things," eventually asserting themselves despite our preferences or biases.

Our challenge today is to be people who love truth more than comfort, who seek understanding rather than mere confirmation, who speak honestly even when silence would be easier, and who build lives and communities founded on the solid rock of God's word rather than the shifting sands of cultural opinion.

When God said, "Let there be light," chaos and darkness could not prevail against his word. Similarly, when believers stand firmly and speak God's truth today, the chaos and darkness of our cultural moment cannot ultimately triumph. This confidence empowers us to persevere in truth-telling despite opposition, knowing that we align ourselves with ultimate reality when we align with God's word.

Implementation: Becoming a Guardian of Truth in a Post-Truth World

1. **Personal truth audit:** Examine your life for areas where you might be compromising with falsehood, even in small ways. Consider your speech patterns, social media presence, financial practices, and workplace behavior. Commit to alignment with truth in every area.
2. **Media discernment practice:** For one month, maintain a journal documenting questionable claims in mainstream news sources. Research each claim using primary sources and multiple

perspectives. Note patterns of bias, emotional manipulation, or selective reporting you discover.

3. **Scripture saturation plan:** Develop a systematic approach to immersing yourself in God's word beyond occasional reading. This might include memorization of key passages about truth, listening to audio scripture during commutes, joining a bible study focused on applying scripture to current issues, or scheduling dedicated daily time for deeper study.
4. **Truth-speaking preparation:** Identify three truths you believe need to be spoken in your sphere of influence. For each, prepare three versions: a gentle, private conversation approach; a firm but respectful public declaration; and a concise social media or written statement. Practice each version, anticipating potential responses.
5. **Alternative ecosystem support:** Evaluate the media, educational resources, and cultural content you consume and financially support. Intentionally redirect at least a portion of your time and resources toward alternatives committed to biblical truth and factual accuracy. This might include Christian education, truthful media outlets, or content creators who demonstrate integrity.

Chapter 10: The Lucifer Virus and Christ's Antidote

In our increasingly technological world, we've become familiar with the concept of viral infections—not just biological ones that attack our bodies, but digital viruses that corrupt our computers and systems. When a virus infiltrates a computer, it doesn't announce its presence with flashing warnings. Instead, it works quietly in the background, subtly altering code, corrupting files, and redirecting functions to serve its own purposes rather than the user's.

This technological metaphor helps us understand the spiritual reality first introduced in the Garden of Eden—what I call the "Lucifer virus." When Satan tempted Eve, he didn't present himself as an enemy of God but as one offering enhanced wisdom: "You will be like God, knowing good and evil" (Genesis 3:5). This initial deception infected humanity with a spiritual virus that has been passed down through generations.

The Lucifer virus fundamentally corrupts human nature, redirecting our spiritual code away from its original divine design. Just as a computer virus might make your device behave erratically or contrary to its intended purpose, this spiritual infection causes humans to consistently choose patterns that lead to destruction rather than flourishing.

This infection manifests in three primary symptoms—the very crimes that characterized both Lucifer's fall and Barabbas's guilt: insurrection, rebellion, and murder.

Insurrection represents the attempt to overthrow legitimate authority. Lucifer wasn't content with his exalted position as the "anointed cherub who covers" but sought to ascend above his station: "I will ascend to heaven; I will raise my throne above the stars of God... I will make myself like the Most High" (Isaiah 14:13-14). This insurrectionist spirit infects humanity whenever we seek to place ourselves above divinely established authority.

Rebellion goes beyond mere disobedience to active resistance against rightful rule. While insurrection seeks to replace authority, rebellion seeks to reject it altogether.

Lucifer's declaration, "I will not serve," epitomizes this spirit that rejects submission even when beneficial. This rebellious infection manifests in humanity's resistance to God's commands—not because they harm us but simply because they limit our autonomy.

Murder represents the ultimate destruction of what God has created and values. Jesus identified Satan as "a murderer from the beginning" (John 8:44). This murderous aspect of the infection expresses itself not just in literal killing but in all forms of destruction—of truth through lying, of reputation through slander, of unity through division, of purity through corruption.

These three symptoms—insurrection, rebellion, and murder—characterize all manifestations of evil in our world. Whether examining personal sin, cultural degradation, or political tyranny, we find these elements consistently present. The Barabbas bias is simply our natural affinity for these infected patterns when our spiritual immune system remains compromised.

The pervasiveness of this infection explains why humanity consistently makes self-destructive choices that seem irrational on the surface. The crowd choosing a violent insurrectionist over a healing teacher wasn't making a reasoned decision but responding according to their infected nature. Similarly, societies that reject proven principles of flourishing for experimental arrangements that consistently fail aren't acting rationally but according to this viral programming.

What makes this infection particularly dangerous is that, like many viruses, it has the ability to disguise itself as part of the normal operating system. The infected person doesn't realize they're infected. They believe their thoughts, preferences, and choices originate from their own rational deliberation rather than from a corrupted spiritual code.

This is why Jesus emphasized the absolute necessity of spiritual rebirth. When he told Nicodemus, "Very truly I tell you, no one can see the kingdom of God unless they are born again" (John 3:3), he wasn't establishing an arbitrary religious requirement but addressing a fundamental spiritual reality. Without regeneration, our spiritual perception remains compromised by this infection.

The context of this statement is particularly revealing. Just before introducing the concept of rebirth, Jesus explained it using the Old Testament story of the bronze serpent: "Just as Moses lifted up the snake in the wilderness, so the

Son of Man must be lifted up, that everyone who believes may have eternal life" (John 3:14-15).

This reference to Numbers 21 provides crucial insight into both the infection and its cure. When venomous snakes bit the Israelites in the wilderness, introducing deadly poison into their systems, God instructed Moses to make a bronze serpent and place it on a pole. Anyone who looked at this bronze serpent would live despite being infected with fatal venom.

Bronze in scripture consistently symbolizes judgment. The serpent represents sin and its originator, Satan. By placing a bronze serpent on a pole, God was providing a prophetic picture of Christ's work on the cross. Jesus didn't merely take our sins upon himself—he became sin. As Paul explains, "God made him who had no sin to be sin for us, so that in him we might become the righteousness of God" (2 Corinthians 5:21).

This distinction is crucial. If Jesus had merely carried our sins while remaining separate from them, he would have been like a hazmat worker carrying toxic waste—contaminated on the outside but not internally transformed. Instead, he actually became sin itself, taking not just the penalty but the very nature of sin into himself to break its power.

Just as the bronze serpent on the pole represented God's judgment on the venom killing the Israelites, Christ on the cross represented God's judgment on the Lucifer virus infecting humanity. By becoming sin and then conquering it through resurrection, Jesus created the ultimate antivirus program—a spiritual remedy that can completely transform our corrupted nature.

The genius of this solution addresses the fundamental problem of the infection. The Lucifer virus didn't just affect our external behaviors but rewrote our spiritual DNA. Therefore, forgiveness alone wouldn't be sufficient. We needed complete regeneration—a new birth that would replace our corrupted spiritual code with divine nature.

This is precisely what occurs when we are born again. The Holy Spirit—whom Jesus called the Spirit of Truth, in direct contrast to Satan as the father of lies—enters our being and begins a fundamental recoding of our spiritual DNA. Peter describes this transformation as becoming "participants in the divine nature" (2 Peter 1:4).

This spiritual recoding doesn't happen instantaneously in our experience, though it is complete in God's perspective. Like any robust antivirus program, the Spirit's work methodically addresses infected areas of our being through a process scripture calls sanctification. The infection remains present in what Paul calls "the flesh" or "the old self," while the cure works through "the Spirit" or "the new self."

This explains the internal conflict believers experience—what Paul describes as two opposing laws at war within us (Romans 7:23). The Lucifer virus continues attempting to corrupt our system, while the divine antivirus continually works to detect and heal these infections.

What makes Christ's antidote so powerful is that it directly counteracts the three primary symptoms of the Lucifer virus:

Against **insurrection**, Christ offers submission. While Satan said, "I will ascend," Jesus "made himself nothing by taking the very nature of a servant... he humbled himself by becoming obedient to death—even death on a cross" (Philippians 2:7-8). This pattern of humble submission represents the new coding that replaces insurrectionist tendencies in believers.

Against **rebellion**, Christ offers obedience. While Satan said, "I will not serve," Jesus declared, "I have come down from heaven not to do my will but to do the will of him who sent me" (John 6:38). This perfect alignment with the

Father's will provides the new template that counters our rebellious programming.

Against **murder**, Christ offers self-sacrifice. While Satan seeks to destroy what God values, Jesus gave himself to preserve what God loves. "Greater love has no one than this: to lay down one's life for one's friends" (John 15:13). This sacrificial love replaces destructive impulses with life-giving service.

Understanding this viral infection and its antidote helps explain why unregenerate humanity consistently manifests the Barabbas bias. Without spiritual rebirth, people remain under the influence of their corrupted programming, naturally gravitating toward patterns of insurrection, rebellion, and destruction while rejecting patterns of submission, obedience, and sacrifice.

This understanding also explains why spiritually reborn believers sometimes still manifest aspects of the Barabbas bias. Though fundamentally healed, we remain in a process of having our minds renewed (Romans 12:2) and putting to death the misdeeds of the body (Romans 8:13). The divine antivirus is completely effective, but its application throughout our being requires cooperative participation.

The battle between the Lucifer virus and Christ's antidote manifests not just individually but collectively in our culture. Educational systems, media narratives, entertainment, and political movements often serve as transmission vectors for the infection. Consider how many modern educational philosophies privilege student autonomy over received wisdom, how entertainment glorifies rebellion against authority, and how political movements often celebrate insurrection against established order.

Conversely, institutions and movements aligned with Christ's antidote emphasize values like service over self-promotion, responsibility over rights, sacrifice over self-fulfillment, and truth over preference. These countercultural patterns directly challenge the viral programming of our age.

During the COVID pandemic, we saw this battle play out dramatically. The Lucifer virus manifested in authoritarian overreach that sought control rather than genuine public health, in censorship that suppressed truth rather than protecting from misinformation, and in protocols that often caused more harm than healing. Christ's antidote manifested in sacrificial service to the vulnerable, in courage to speak truth despite consequences, and in communities that maintained human connection when isolation was mandated.

This same battle continues in every significant cultural and political conflict of our time. Behind disagreements about policies and practices lie deeper spiritual alignments with either the viral infection of Lucifer or the healing antidote of Christ.

Understanding this spiritual reality transforms how we view human behavior and cultural trends. People captured by the Barabbas bias aren't merely making poor choices but are responding according to corrupted programming they cannot recognize without spiritual regeneration. This should inspire compassion rather than mere condemnation. As Jesus prayed from the cross, "Father, forgive them, for they do not know what they are doing" (Luke 23:34).

At the same time, this understanding should strengthen our resolve to proclaim Christ's antidote. If the fundamental problem is spiritual infection, the solution must be spiritual transformation. Political activism, educational reform, and cultural engagement have their place, but without accompanying spiritual renewal, they merely treat symptoms rather than addressing the root cause.

The contemporary quest for social justice without spiritual regeneration illustrates this limitation. Many genuinely seek to address inequities and abuses but do so through frameworks infected with the same virus they aim to combat. Rejecting divine authority while seeking human justice inevitably produces new forms of oppression rather than true liberation. As history repeatedly demonstrates, revolutions without spiritual transformation merely exchange one form of corruption for another.

This pattern reflects a deeper spiritual principle: self-loathing and projection. The Lucifer virus produces an unconscious self-hatred that gets projected onto others. Those infected don't recognize their own corruption but fiercely condemn it in others. Jesus addressed this dynamic when he asked, "Why do you look at the speck of sawdust in your brother's eye and pay no attention to the plank in your own eye?" (Matthew 7:3).

This projection explains why the most vocal advocates for certain causes often privately violate the very principles they publicly champion. The crusader against corruption who engages in secret graft, the sexual purity campaigner hiding his own pornography addiction, the environmental activist with an enormous carbon footprint—these contradictions aren't merely hypocrisy but manifestations of unrecognized self-loathing.

Christ's antidote addresses this dynamic by first transforming our relationship with ourselves. When we receive God's love and forgiveness, we can begin to properly love ourselves as bearers of divine image. This healthy self-love then extends naturally to others: "Love your neighbor as yourself" (Mark 12:31). Without being healed in our self-perception, we cannot maintain healthy relationships with others.

This healing process begins with acknowledging our infection—what scripture calls confession of sin. Just as a patient must recognize their illness before accepting treatment, we must acknowledge our spiritual corruption before embracing Christ's cure. This confession isn't merely admitting specific wrong actions but recognizing our fundamental condition as spiritually infected beings in need of complete regeneration.

The depth of this infection explains why mere moral reform proves insufficient. Behavior modification might temporarily suppress symptoms but cannot address the underlying viral code. This is why religious systems based on rule-keeping ultimately fail to transform human nature. They attempt to manage the infection through external constraints rather than providing internal healing.

Christ's antidote, by contrast, works from inside out. It begins with spiritual regeneration—the impartation of divine life that creates a new spiritual identity. This new nature then progressively manifests in transformed thinking, desires, and behaviors. As Jesus explained, "Make a tree good and its fruit will be good" (Matthew 12:33). Change the root, and the fruit changes naturally.

This transformational process requires both divine initiative and human cooperation. God provides the antidote—we cannot create it ourselves. Yet we must actively appropriate and apply this cure through what scripture calls "working out your salvation" (Philippians 2:12). This collaborative process involves spiritual disciplines, community support, and intentional alignment with truth.

Perhaps the most powerful aspect of Christ's antidote is its effect on our ability to love. The Lucifer virus fundamentally distorts love, replacing it with various counterfeits: possessiveness masquerading as protection, codependency disguised as devotion, exploitation presenting as appreciation. These distortions explain why even our attempts at love often produce harm rather than healing.

The divine antidote restores our capacity for genuine love by first connecting us to its source. "We love because he first loved us" (1 John 4:19). When we experience God's unconditional love—a love not based on our performance, appearance, or usefulness—we gain both the pattern and power for loving others authentically.

This transformed capacity for love becomes the most convincing evidence of spiritual healing. Jesus identified this as the distinguishing mark of his followers: "By this everyone will know that you are my disciples, if you love one another" (John 13:35). Not doctrinal precision, religious observance, or moral perfection, but love itself becomes the ultimate proof of Christ's antidote at work.

During my own journey, I've witnessed this healing process transform the most unlikely individuals. Former drug addicts whose self-destructive patterns seemed irreversible. Hardened criminals whose violent tendencies appeared engraved in their character. Bitter, hate-filled individuals whose capacity for love seemed permanently corrupted. In each case, Christ's antidote proved more powerful than the viral infection that had dominated their lives.

I've also observed this transformation in my own family. When I became a Christian as a young man obsessed with surfing and self-gratification, my mother noticed an immediate difference in my character. My formerly dismissive and self-centered treatment of her was replaced by genuine care and respect. This tangible change convinced her of the reality of spiritual transformation more than any theological argument could have. Within months, she too embraced Christ, followed later by my brother.

This pattern of transformation spreading through relationships illustrates another aspect of Christ's antidote: it's contagious in the best possible way. While the Lucifer virus spreads through deception and corruption, Christ's cure spreads through authentic demonstration of its effects. As others witness genuine transformation, they become open to its possibility in their own lives.

The most powerful response to the Barabbas bias in our culture isn't angry condemnation but compelling demonstration of the alternative. When people encounter genuine love, integrity, peace, and purpose in believers, they glimpse what spiritual health looks like. This lived testimony often opens doors that arguments alone cannot.

As we conclude this chapter, remember that the greatest evidence for Christ's antidote is your own transformed life.

When Christ heals your spiritual DNA, you become what Paul calls "a letter from Christ... written not with ink but with the Spirit of the living God, not on tablets of stone but on tablets of human hearts" (2 Corinthians 3:3). Your life becomes a visible testimony to the invisible reality of spiritual healing.

In a world infected with the Lucifer virus, you carry the cure. Share it not just through proclamation but through demonstration—allowing others to see what spiritual health looks like in human form. In doing so, you participate in God's ongoing mission to heal a virus-stricken world through the ultimate antidote found in Christ.

Implementation: Allowing God's Love to Heal Your Spiritual DNA

1. **Infection-recognition practice:** Identify specific manifestations of the Lucifer virus (insurrection, rebellion, destruction) in your thoughts, behaviors, and relationships. Journal about how these patterns developed and how they affect your spiritual health.
2. **Antidote-application exercise:** For each identified infection, study and meditate on the corresponding aspect of Christ's character (submission,

obedience, self-sacrifice). Create specific practices that cultivate these qualities in your daily life.

3. **Love-flow assessment:** Evaluate areas where your capacity to receive and give love might be blocked. Consider whether you truly believe God loves you unconditionally, whether you've genuinely accepted yourself, and how these factors affect your ability to love others.
4. **Self-loathing identification:** Through prayer and reflection, identify beliefs about yourself that might stem from the infection rather than truth. For each negative belief, research and memorize a corresponding scriptural affirmation of your value and identity in Christ.
5. **Contagious-healing inventory:** List individuals in your sphere of influence who might be receptive to Christ's healing. Rather than planning direct evangelism, develop specific ways to demonstrate the effects of spiritual health in your interactions with them—showing rather than telling about the antidote's power.

Chapter 11: Seeing with New Eyes

When Jesus encountered Nicodemus—a man of impressive religious credentials and sincere spiritual seeking—He made a statement that must have bewildered this learned teacher: "Very truly I tell you, no one can see the kingdom of God unless they are born again" (John 3:3). Notice the specific language Jesus used. He didn't say no one can enter the kingdom without rebirth, but that no one can even see it.

This distinction reveals something profound about spiritual perception. The kingdom of God isn't merely a future reality we'll enter after death but a present reality surrounding us that remains invisible to unregenerate humanity. Without spiritual rebirth, we're like blind people in an art gallery—surrounded by beauty we cannot perceive.

This blindness explains why the Barabbas bias persists despite its destructive consequences. People don't choose rebellion, chaos, and death because they consciously prefer these outcomes but because they cannot see the superior alternatives. The crowd shouting "Give us Barabbas!" couldn't perceive the divine reality standing before them in Christ. They weren't making an informed choice between alternatives they clearly understood but responding according to their limited perception.

Spiritual blindness has several characteristics that make it particularly dangerous:

First, the spiritually blind don't know they're blind. Unlike physical blindness, which is immediately apparent to those who suffer from it, spiritual blindness includes the inability to recognize one's condition. Jesus addressed this when He told the Pharisees, "If you were blind, you would not be guilty of sin; but now that you claim you can see, your guilt remains" (John 9:41). The most dangerous aspect of spiritual blindness is the delusion of sight.

Second, spiritual blindness is selective rather than total. The unregenerate person can perceive physical reality accurately while completely missing spiritual dimensions of the same reality. They can analyze economic data, technological specifications, or scientific findings with precision while remaining oblivious to the moral and spiritual implications of these same facts. This partial sight creates the illusion of comprehensive understanding.

Third, spiritual blindness is often accompanied by false illumination. Satan, who "masquerades as an angel of light" (2 Corinthians 11:14), provides counterfeit enlightenment that appears to explain reality while actually leading further from truth. This explains why highly educated and intelligent people can be utterly deceived in spiritual matters—their intellectual light becomes darkness when disconnected from divine illumination.

Fourth, spiritual blindness tends to be progressive rather than static. Jesus described this progression: "They are blind guides. If the blind lead the blind, both will fall into a pit" (Matthew 15:14). One deception leads to another in a downward spiral that encompasses ever-larger portions of perception. What begins as blindness in one area gradually extends to others.

Understanding these characteristics helps explain why rational arguments often fail to persuade people captivated by the Barabbas bias. We aren't merely dealing with misinformation that can be corrected with better data but with a fundamental perceptual disability that distorts how all information is processed.

This is precisely why Jesus emphasized spiritual rebirth as the necessary precondition for spiritual sight. No amount of education, argumentation, or evidence can overcome spiritual blindness. Only divine intervention—the miraculous work of the Holy Spirit generating new life—can restore our capacity to perceive spiritual reality accurately.

When spiritual rebirth occurs, it's like the healing of the man born blind in John 9. His progressive experience—moving from total blindness to seeing people "like trees walking around" to eventually seeing clearly—mirrors the journey of many believers. Spiritual sight doesn't typically arrive fully formed but develops through stages of increasing clarity.

This progressive nature of spiritual perception explains why even regenerate believers sometimes manifest aspects of the Barabbas bias. Though fundamentally healed, our spiritual vision continues to sharpen throughout our lifetime. Areas where our sight remains dim correspond to areas where our choices may still align with old patterns rather than divine reality.

The Bible uses several metaphors to describe this perceptual transformation. Paul speaks of a "veil" being removed when one turns to the Lord (2 Corinthians 3:16). Jesus describes it as recovery of sight for the blind (Luke 4:18). The Psalmist declares, "In your light we see light" (Psalm 36:9), suggesting that divine illumination is necessary to perceive light properly.

Each of these metaphors emphasizes that spiritual perception isn't achieved through human effort but received as divine gift. We cannot remove our own spiritual cataracts or lift the veil that obscures our vision. Only divine intervention can restore our capacity to see reality as it truly is.

This divine restoration of sight begins with recognizing our blindness—acknowledging that our natural perceptual capacities are insufficient for spiritual reality. Jesus warned, "Those who see will become blind" (John 9:39), indicating that presumption of sight actually prevents true vision. Only when we acknowledge our blindness do we become candidates for healing.

Once we recognize our need for divine illumination, the Holy Spirit—whom Jesus called the Spirit of Truth—begins the process of perceptual restoration. This involves several dimensions:

First, the Spirit illuminates scripture, transforming it from mere religious text to living divine communication. The disciples on the road to Emmaus experienced this when Jesus "opened their minds so they could understand the Scriptures" (Luke 24:45). Without this illumination, even direct exposure to biblical content leaves one spiritually uninformed.

Second, the Spirit provides discernment about current events and circumstances, revealing their spiritual significance beyond surface appearances. Paul describes this as having "the mind of Christ" (1 Corinthians 2:16)—an ability to interpret reality from divine perspective rather than merely human viewpoint.

Third, the Spirit grants insight into human motives and conditions, enabling us to see beyond behaviors to underlying spiritual realities. This explains how Jesus could perceive thoughts and intentions that weren't verbally expressed. While we don't possess His perfect discernment, the Spirit provides growing capacity to discern spiritual conditions in ourselves and others.

Fourth, the Spirit reveals the presence and activity of spiritual forces—both divine and demonic—operating behind visible circumstances. Paul prayed that believers would have "the eyes of your heart enlightened"

(Ephesians 1:18) to perceive realities invisible to natural sight. This supernatural perception doesn't replace natural observation but adds an essential dimension to it.

These aspects of spiritual sight develop progressively as we cultivate sensitivity to the Spirit's illumination. Like any faculty, spiritual perception strengthens with use and atrophies with neglect. This explains why some mature believers demonstrate remarkable discernment while some new believers—though genuinely reborn—still manifest significant perceptual limitations.

The development of spiritual sight requires certain practices and conditions:

First, immersion in scripture provides the necessary framework for spiritual perception. The Bible isn't merely a source of information but a lens through which we learn to see all reality. Regular, thoughtful engagement with scripture trains our spiritual perception to recognize patterns and principles we would otherwise miss.

Second, prayer—particularly listening prayer—attunes us to the Spirit's voice and illumination. While many believers focus exclusively on speaking to God, developing spiritual sight requires learning to recognize God's communication to us through various means.

Third, community with other believers provides complementary perspectives that compensate for our individual blind spots. No single believer sees perfectly, but the body of Christ collectively perceives more completely than any individual member. Isolation invariably distorts our spiritual vision.

Fourth, obedience to revealed truth increases capacity for further illumination. Jesus taught that faithfulness with little leads to entrustment with much (Luke 16:10). Similarly, acting on the light we've received opens us to greater illumination, while disobedience progressively dims our spiritual sight.

Fifth, purity of heart removes internal distortions that cloud perception. Jesus taught, "Blessed are the pure in heart, for they will see God" (Matthew 5:8). Moral compromise, unforgiveness, pride, and other heart conditions function like cataracts that blur spiritual vision regardless of external illumination.

During the COVID pandemic, I witnessed dramatic differences in perceptual clarity among believers. Some immediately discerned the spiritual dimensions of unfolding events, recognizing patterns of deception and control beneath surface narratives. Others, though sincere in faith, seemed unable to perceive beyond official explanations, accepting increasingly implausible narratives without question.

This perceptual divergence wasn't primarily intellectual but spiritual. Many highly educated believers demonstrated remarkable blindness, while some with limited formal education showed extraordinary discernment. The difference wasn't IQ but developed capacity for spiritual sight—the ability to recognize patterns of heaven versus patterns of hell operating in current events.

The same divergence appears in every significant cultural conflict. Some believers immediately discern spiritual forces operating behind political movements, educational philosophies, entertainment trends, and technological developments. Others perceive only surface features, missing the deeper spiritual currents shaping these phenomena.

This perceptual difference explains why Christians often respond differently to the same cultural developments. Where one believer sees a demonic assault requiring opposition, another sees merely human progress requiring adaptation. Where one discerns a heaven-inspired movement deserving support, another perceives only political or social change without spiritual significance.

These different perceptions often lead to painful divisions within the body of Christ. During COVID, churches split over pandemic responses, with sincere believers on both sides convinced they were seeing clearly while their brothers and sisters were blind. Similar divisions occur regarding political alignments, cultural engagement strategies, and responses to various social movements.

How should we navigate these perceptual differences among believers? Several principles can guide us:

First, recognize that spiritual sight develops progressively in all believers. None of us sees perfectly or completely. This humility should temper our confidence in our own perceptions while increasing our willingness to consider alternative perspectives.

Second, prioritize unity with other believers even amid perceptual differences. Paul urged the Romans to "accept one another, then, just as Christ accepted you" (Romans 15:7) despite significant differences in spiritual perception regarding food, days, and other practices.

Third, focus on clear scriptural teaching rather than disputed perceptions when determining fellowship boundaries. Where scripture speaks explicitly, we stand firmly; where perceptions diverge on matters scripture doesn't directly address, we extend grace and maintain relationship.

Fourth, continue developing your own spiritual sight through the practices mentioned earlier. Rather than assuming others must change their perception to match yours, focus on refining your own vision through scripture, prayer, community, obedience, and heart purity.

Fifth, recognize that different members of Christ's body may be given different perceptual assignments. Just as physical eyes focus on different portions of the visual field to create comprehensive vision, different believers may be assigned to monitor different aspects of spiritual reality for the body's benefit.

Beyond these principles for navigating differences among believers, we must also consider how to engage with those who remain spiritually blind—the unregenerate who cannot yet see spiritual reality due to their unredeemed condition.

The primary response must be compassion rather than condemnation. Jesus looked at the crowds and "had compassion on them, because they were harassed and helpless, like sheep without a shepherd" (Matthew 9:36). Their blindness made them victims before it made them culpable. The appropriate response to a blind person walking toward danger isn't anger but assistance.

This compassion should manifest in prayer for divine illumination. Paul wrote that "the god of this age has blinded the minds of unbelievers, so that they cannot see the light of the gospel" (2 Corinthians 4:4). Since spiritual blindness has supernatural origins, its cure requires supernatural intervention. No human argument, however brilliant, can substitute for the Spirit's illuminating work.

Our engagement should also involve patient explanation rather than frustrated dismissal. Peter urged believers to "always be prepared to give an answer to everyone who asks you to give the reason for the hope that you have. But do this with gentleness and respect" (1 Peter 3:15). We offer perspectives the spiritually blind cannot yet see, but we do so with understanding of their perceptual limitations.

Most importantly, we must recognize that demonstration often succeeds where explanation fails. When the blind man in John 9 was questioned about his healing, he couldn't explain the theological implications but simply testified, "One thing I do know. I was blind but now I see!" (John 9:25). The tangible transformation in our lives—peace amid chaos, love amid hatred, integrity amid corruption—often communicates spiritual reality more effectively than any verbal explanation.

As we navigate an increasingly dark cultural landscape, the development of spiritual sight becomes not merely beneficial but essential. Jesus warned that in the last days, deception would become so sophisticated that "even the elect" might be deceived if that were possible (Matthew 24:24). Only developed spiritual perception can enable us to recognize and resist such deception.

This heightened perceptual clarity doesn't come automatically with spiritual rebirth but requires intentional development. Like the disciples who initially failed to recognize the risen Christ on the road to Emmaus, many believers possess the capacity for spiritual sight without fully activating it. Their eyes are "restrained" (Luke 24:16) not by divine withholding but by undeveloped perceptual skills.

The journey from blindness to sight, from unconscious bias to conscious choice, from being manipulated by the Barabbas pattern to aligning with Christ's kingdom, begins with a simple prayer: "Lord, open my eyes that I may see" (cf. Psalm 119:18). This humble acknowledgment of our need for divine illumination initiates the process that transforms not just what we see but how we see.

As your spiritual sight develops, you'll begin to recognize both the Barabbas bias and the Christ pattern in places you previously missed them. News that once seemed merely political will reveal spiritual dimensions. Entertainment that appeared innocuous will display subtle messages either aligned with or opposed to divine reality. Relationships will reveal spiritual currents operating beneath surface interactions.

This growing perception doesn't make us paranoid but properly discerning—able to "test the spirits to see whether they are from God" (1 John 4:1). Rather than seeing demons behind every bush, mature spiritual sight distinguishes between ordinary human failings and genuinely supernatural opposition, between cultural trends with spiritual significance and those without it.

The ultimate goal of spiritual sight isn't merely accurate perception of evil but transformative vision of God himself. As John wrote, "We know that when Christ appears, we shall be like him, for we shall see him as he is" (1 John 3:2). Seeing Christ clearly transforms us into His likeness—the ultimate purpose of restored spiritual perception.

This transformative vision begins in this life but reaches completion in eternity. Paul described our current perception as "seeing through a glass, darkly" while anticipating a future when we will see "face to face" (1 Corinthians 13:12 KJV). Even the most developed spiritual sight in this life remains partial and imperfect, yet it provides essential guidance for navigating a world infected with the Barabbas bias.

As you continue developing your spiritual perception, remember that the goal isn't merely to see what's wrong with the world but to envision what could be right with it. Prophetic perception includes both recognition of current corruption and revelation of potential restoration. We see both the world as it is in its fallen condition and the world as it could be through redemptive transformation.

This dual perception enables us to engage cultural challenges with both realism about present darkness and hope for future light. We neither succumb to naive optimism that ignores genuine evil nor surrender to cynical pessimism that denies redemptive possibility. Instead, with spiritually enlightened eyes, we see both the depth of the problem and the height of the potential solution.

In practical terms, this balanced perception enables us to address the Barabbas bias without either underestimating its power or overestimating its permanence. We recognize its pervasive influence while confidently proclaiming and demonstrating its antidote. We neither pretend the infection doesn't exist nor believe it cannot be healed.

This balanced spiritual sight represents the mature perception Jesus desires for His followers—eyes that see both the tares and the wheat growing together, both the leaven working through the dough and the pearl of great price worth everything to obtain. Such comprehensive perception enables effective engagement with our world that neither retreats from its challenges nor conforms to its patterns.

Implementation: Practicing Spiritual Discernment in Everyday Situations

1. **Media perception practice:** Select a popular news story, film, or music release. After experiencing it, journal about both its surface content and potential spiritual significance. Look for patterns aligned with either the Barabbas bias (rebellion, self-exaltation, destruction) or Christ's kingdom (submission, service, creation). Compare your perceptions with other spiritually mature believers.

2. **Pattern recognition training:** Create a two-column document with "Patterns of Heaven" and "Patterns of Hell" as headings. Throughout one week, record examples of each pattern you observe in daily life—in conversations, media, work situations, family dynamics, etc. Review weekly to strengthen your ability to recognize these patterns instantly.
3. **Blind spot identification:** Ask three spiritually mature people who know you well: "Where might my spiritual perception be underdeveloped or distorted?" Receive their observations without defensiveness, looking for consistent patterns in their feedback. Create a specific plan to address identified blind spots.
4. **Scripture-immersion experiment:** Choose one book of the Bible (a gospel or epistle works well) and read it daily for 30 days. After each reading, note new insights that weren't apparent in previous readings. Watch how repeated exposure to the same scripture progressively illuminates aspects you initially missed.
5. **Perception-purification exercise:** Identify emotional responses that might distort your spiritual perception—fear, anger, pride, desire for approval, etc. For each one, develop a specific prayer that surrenders this emotion to God before

attempting to discern situations where it might influence your perception.

Chapter 12: The Love Revolution

In our journey through the Barabbas bias, we've explored its manifestations in politics, culture, and individual psychology. We've examined biblical patterns that reveal its ancient roots and modern expressions. We've considered how spiritual blindness perpetuates this bias and how renewed perception helps overcome it. Now we arrive at the ultimate antidote to this pervasive spiritual infection: a revolution of divine love.

Love isn't merely one solution among many but the fundamental answer to humanity's deepest problems. The Barabbas bias—our tendency to choose rebellion, self-exaltation, and destruction—ultimately stems from love deficiency. Where genuine love flourishes, this bias cannot maintain its grip. As John wrote, "Perfect love drives out fear" (1 John 4:18), and fear lies at the root of the Barabbas bias—fear that manifests as rage, control, and destruction.

To understand how love overcomes this bias, we must first understand the nature of genuine love. In Hebrew thought, love isn't primarily a feeling but a commitment that produces action. When God revealed Himself to Moses as "abounding in steadfast love" (Exodus 34:6), He was describing not an emotion but a faithful commitment to covenant relationship that manifests in consistent action for our good.

This understanding differs dramatically from contemporary concepts of love as primarily emotional or sentimental. Biblical love encompasses feelings but transcends them—remaining steadfast even when emotions fluctuate. It's this steadfast, action-oriented love that provides the ultimate answer to the chaos, division, and destruction produced by the Barabbas bias.

The revolutionary power of divine love begins with understanding God as the all-sufficient source. When God revealed Himself to Abraham, He used the name El Shaddai, which means "the all-sufficient one" or more literally, "the all-sufficient source from whom all things derive." This revelation transformed Abraham's understanding of both God and himself.

At 99 years old, with a body described in Romans 4 as "as good as dead," Abraham received a new identity through this revelation. God changed his name from Abram ("exalted father") to Abraham ("father of multitudes"), inserting part of His own name (the Hebrew letter "h," representing breath) into Abraham's identity. This divine insertion enabled life to flow where death had reigned, culminating in the miraculous birth of Isaac despite Abraham and Sarah's advanced age.

This pattern reveals a profound spiritual principle: when God puts Himself into our identity, He transforms our natural limitations into channels for supernatural provision. Our insufficiency becomes the stage for His all-sufficiency. Our weakness becomes the context for His strength. Our emptiness becomes the vessel for His fullness.

This indwelling of divine all-sufficiency creates what I call the "fountain effect"—an internal source of love that continually flows regardless of external circumstances. Jesus described this phenomenon: "Whoever believes in me, as Scripture has said, rivers of living water will flow from within them" (John 7:38). Not a stagnant pond depending on rainfall but a flowing river with an internal source.

This fountain effect represents the most powerful answer to the Barabbas bias in both individuals and societies. When we operate from internal abundance rather than perceived scarcity, we no longer feel compelled to grasp, control, and destroy. Instead, we naturally extend to others what we've abundantly received.

Consider how this principle applied in my own experience: When I first encountered Christ as a young surfer in Australia, my life revolved around self-gratification and self-promotion. Though I wouldn't have recognized it then, I was operating from internal emptiness—a love deficiency that manifested in self-centered behaviors.

After my conversion, my mother quickly noticed the difference. The self-centered son who had treated her dismissively was replaced by someone who demonstrated genuine care and appreciation. This transformation wasn't the result of behavior modification or rule-following but of internal abundance. Having received God's unconditional love, I had something to give that wasn't dependent on my own limited resources.

This transformation proved more persuasive than any theological argument. Within months, my mother herself embraced Christ, followed later by my brother. They saw in me something they wanted for themselves—not a new religion but a new capacity for love that flowed from an inexhaustible source.

The power of this love revolution extends beyond personal relationships to transform communities, institutions, and eventually nations. Throughout history, genuine Christian love has created counter-cultures that demonstrate alternatives to the dominant patterns of rebellion, selfishness, and exploitation.

Early Christians astonished the Roman world by caring for plague victims (including non-Christians) when others fled, by rescuing abandoned infants when infanticide was common practice, by treating slaves as brothers and sisters when slavery was unquestioned, and by sharing resources freely when accumulation was the norm. This radically different way of living flowed not from superior ethics but from an internal transformation—the fountain effect of divine love.

Similar counter-cultures have emerged throughout history whenever believers have experienced and expressed this revolutionary love. From the monastic communities that preserved learning and served the poor during Europe's darkest periods to the abolitionist movements that confronted institutionalized cruelty, from civil rights advocates who insisted on loving enemies to contemporary ministries serving the most marginalized—each demonstrates love's power to create alternatives to the Barabbas patterns of their time.

During the COVID pandemic, I witnessed this love revolution creating a counter-culture within our own church community. While fear dominated mainstream narratives and many institutions sacrificed human connection for perceived safety, our congregation maintained bonds of community. We created spaces where people could gather, worship, and support one another despite external pressures to isolate.

We witnessed the fountain effect as people who had received care extended it to others—delivering groceries to the vulnerable, providing financial assistance to those who lost income, offering emotional support during unprecedented stress, and maintaining human touch when physical contact was discouraged. These weren't programmatic initiatives but spontaneous expressions of internal abundance.

The most powerful testimony came from medical professionals within our congregation who worked directly with COVID patients. Despite exhaustion and stress, they reported that the internal fountain of God's love sustained them when natural resources were depleted. They discovered they could extend compassion even in the most challenging circumstances because they were drawing from an inexhaustible source.

This experience highlighted a crucial aspect of the love revolution: it thrives precisely when natural conditions would suggest its impossibility. Just as Abraham's dead body became the context for God's life-giving power, our limitations become the canvas for displaying divine all-sufficiency. The darker the circumstances, the more brightly authentic love shines.

This paradoxical pattern helps explain why persecution and hardship often strengthen rather than weaken genuine Christianity. External opposition can actually intensify internal dependence on the divine fountain, producing more abundant expressions of supernatural love. As Paul discovered, when we are weak, then we are strong (2 Corinthians 12:10)—not through self-effort but through accessing God's all-sufficient power.

The mechanics of this love revolution deserve closer examination. How exactly does divine love transform our natural tendencies toward the Barabbas bias? Several specific mechanisms operate in this revolutionary process:

First, divine love heals the self-loathing that fuels projection and hatred of others. The Barabbas bias fundamentally stems from an inability to properly love ourselves due to unrecognized shame and guilt. When God's unconditional love penetrates this shame, we can begin to see ourselves as beloved despite our flaws. This healthy self-love then extends naturally to others: "Love your neighbor as yourself" (Mark 12:31).

Second, divine love satisfies the deepest human cravings that drive destructive behaviors. Augustine famously observed, "Our hearts are restless until they rest in You." The relentless pursuit of wealth, power, pleasure, and acclaim—which inevitably involves rebellion against divine limits and exploitation of others—represents misdirected attempts to fill God-shaped emptiness. When divine love fills this emptiness, the compulsive drive behind these destructive patterns diminishes.

Third, divine love provides security that eliminates defensive aggression. Much human cruelty stems not from inherent malice but from perceived vulnerability. We attack because we feel threatened; we control because we fear chaos; we hoard because we anticipate scarcity. When divine love establishes our ultimate security in God's faithful care, these defensive responses become unnecessary, enabling generosity, vulnerability, and open-handed living.

Fourth, divine love breaks cycles of retaliation through forgiveness. The Barabbas pattern perpetuates through endless cycles of offense and counter-offense, wound and counter-wound. Divine love interrupts this cycle through supernatural capacity to absorb injury without returning it—to forgive as we have been forgiven. This breaks chains of generational and social trauma that would otherwise continue indefinitely.

Fifth, divine love restores proper recognition of human worth apart from utilitarian value. The Barabbas bias invariably reduces humans to tools or obstacles rather than image-bearers of God. Divine love restores proper perspective, enabling us to value others for their inherent worth rather than their usefulness to our agendas. This fundamentally alters how we approach relationships, politics, economics, and social structures.

These mechanisms operate progressively as we experience and express divine love, gradually transforming both individual psychology and social dynamics. The revolution doesn't happen overnight but advances steadily as love penetrates deeper layers of our being and extends to wider circles of relationship.

The most vivid demonstration of this revolutionary love appears in Jesus himself—particularly in His response from the cross. Facing the ultimate expression of the Barabbas bias—an innocent man condemned while a guilty man goes free—Jesus doesn't retaliate but prays, "Father, forgive them, for they do not know what they are doing" (Luke 23:34).

This incomprehensible response reveals the nature of divine love more clearly than any theological explanation could. In the moment of greatest injustice, Jesus extends forgiveness rather than condemnation. When most justified in righteous anger, He offers mercy instead. This demonstrates love's revolutionary power to transcend the natural human response patterns that perpetuate cycles of violence and hatred.

Consider what would have happened had Jesus responded differently. Had He called down divine judgment on His persecutors, had He cursed those who crucified Him, had He responded according to justice rather than mercy, the entire redemptive narrative would have collapsed. The revolution of love would have been replaced by merely another cycle of violence, regardless of how justified.

Instead, Jesus demonstrated a fundamentally different pattern—one that absorbs violence without returning it, that offers blessing in response to cursing, that extends forgiveness before repentance is expressed. This pattern doesn't merely resist the Barabbas bias but completely transforms it, replacing its fundamental operating system with an entirely different code.

This revolutionary love becomes available to believers through the indwelling Holy Spirit. Paul describes the "fruit of the Spirit" as "love, joy, peace, forbearance, kindness, goodness, faithfulness, gentleness and self-control" (Galatians 5:22-23)—qualities that directly counter the "acts of the flesh" which include "hatred, discord, jealousy, fits of rage, selfish ambition, dissensions, factions and envy" (Galatians 5:19-21).

Notice that these contrasting qualities aren't presented as behaviors we must manufacture through self-effort but as natural fruit that grows from spiritual connection. Just as an apple tree doesn't strain to produce apples but simply channels the life flowing through it, believers don't generate love through determination but express what flows from divine indwelling.

This distinction explains why many religious efforts to improve human behavior ultimately fail. They attempt to modify the fruit without transforming the root. They impose external standards without addressing internal source. They demand love without providing its fountain. The revolutionary power of genuine Christianity lies precisely in its provision of internal transformation rather than mere external regulation.

During my years in ministry, I've witnessed countless individuals try and fail to love through self-effort, only to discover transformative capacity when they finally experience and receive God's unconditional love. The sequence matters immensely: "We love because he first loved us" (1 John 4:19). Our capacity to love authentically flows from first being loved authentically.

This principle extends beyond individual psychology to social transformation. Many well-intentioned movements seek to establish justice, equality, and compassion through structural changes alone, without addressing the human heart's fundamental condition. These efforts inevitably disappoint because external systems cannot solve internal problems. Without transformed hearts, new systems quickly become tools for old patterns of selfishness and oppression.

Conversely, genuinely transformed individuals begin creating new social patterns regardless of existing structures. Early Christians established radical equality among members despite living within the Roman Empire's rigid hierarchical system. Abolitionists treated enslaved people with dignity long before laws acknowledged their humanity. Civil rights leaders practiced integration before segregation laws were changed. Internal transformation produces external innovation that eventually reshapes wider social patterns.

This doesn't mean structural changes are unnecessary—they often formalize and protect what transformed hearts have already begun practicing. But lasting social transformation begins with revolutions of love within individual hearts, gradually extending to relationships, communities, institutions, and eventually systems.

The love revolution spreads through a combination of proclamation and demonstration. We announce the good news of God's all-sufficient love while simultaneously displaying its effects in tangible ways. Words without demonstration lack credibility; demonstration without explanation lacks clarity. Together, they create compelling invitations to experience this revolutionary love personally.

In practical terms, this means creating environments where divine love can be both explained and experienced. Churches should function as love laboratories where people encounter genuine acceptance while hearing transformative truth. Our worship, fellowship, service, and outreach should all demonstrate the fountain effect—love flowing from abundance rather than obligation.

This revolutionary love isn't soft or sentimental but carries tremendous power. It confronts injustice not from rage but from passionate commitment to human flourishing. It establishes boundaries not from fear but from wisdom about destructive patterns. It speaks truth not from superiority but from devotion to authentic relationship. Love's gentle appearance masks its world-changing strength.

History's greatest revolutions haven't come through superior firepower but through superior love-power. From Jesus's small band of disciples transforming the mighty Roman Empire to Gandhi's nonviolent resistance overcoming British colonialism, from Martin Luther King Jr.'s love-based activism dismantling segregation to Desmond Tutu's truth and reconciliation process healing post-apartheid South Africa—love has repeatedly proven more powerful than violence, coercion, or domination.

The Barabbas bias will ultimately be overcome not through better arguments, stricter laws, or more sophisticated systems, but through a revolution of divine love that transforms human hearts from the inside out. This revolution begins with individual experience of God's all-sufficient love and extends outward in ever-widening circles of transformation.

As we conclude this exploration of the Barabbas bias and its antidote, I invite you to consider your own participation in this love revolution. Have you personally experienced the fountain effect of God's all-sufficient love? Does your life demonstrate the internal abundance that flows regardless of external circumstances? Are you extending to others what you've abundantly received?

If not, the invitation remains open. The fountain flows freely for anyone willing to acknowledge their thirst. The transformation awaits anyone ready to exchange the Barabbas patterns of rebellion, self-exaltation, and destruction for the Christ patterns of submission, service, and creation. The revolution welcomes new participants daily, offering not mere improvement but complete reinvention through divine love.

In a world increasingly dominated by rage, fear, and division—the toxic fruits of the Barabbas bias—this revolution of love offers the only sustainable alternative. Political solutions prove temporary without transformed hearts. Educational reforms fall short without renewed minds. Economic changes disappoint without regenerated values. Only love that flows from divine source can truly and permanently transform human nature and human society.

The ultimate question isn't whether this revolution will succeed—history's trajectory and scripture's promises confirm its eventual triumph. The question is whether we will actively participate in this revolution, becoming channels of divine love in our relationships, communities, workplaces, and wider cultural engagement. The world doesn't need more angry activists but more love revolutionaries who demonstrate alternative patterns to the prevailing Barabbas bias.

As Jesus declared, "By this everyone will know that you are my disciples, if you love one another" (John 13:35). Not by theological precision, political alignment, cultural relevance, or moral perfection, but by love itself. This remains the ultimate apologetic in a world desperate for authentic alternatives to its self-destructive patterns.

May we become living demonstrations of this revolutionary love—not merely discussing the Barabbas bias but embodying its antidote through lives transformed by the all-sufficient fountain of divine love.

Implementation: Becoming a Conduit of God's Transformative Love

1. **Fountain assessment:** Honestly evaluate your current love capacity. Do you give from abundance or scarcity? Does your love flow naturally or require straining effort? When depleted, how quickly does your capacity replenish? Journal about these questions to establish a baseline for measuring growth.
2. **Divine love meditation:** Set aside 15 minutes daily for four weeks to meditate on passages about God's love (e.g., Psalm 103, Romans 8:31-39, 1 John 4:7-21). Rather than analyzing intellectually, imagine yourself receiving this love personally. Visualize it filling every empty space within you and overflowing to others.
3. **Forgiveness inventory:** List individuals who have wounded you, describing both the offense and its impact on you. For each person, pray: "Father, I choose to forgive [name] for [specific action] which made me feel [impact]. I release them from my judgment and entrust them to Your perfect justice

and mercy." Repeat until you sense internal release.

4. **Love laboratory experiment:** Identify one challenging relationship where Barabbas patterns (control, judgment, distance) currently operate. For 30 days, practice specific counter-patterns: blessing instead of criticizing, curiosity instead of assumption, presence instead of avoidance. Document changes in both the relationship and your internal experience.
5. **Abundance activation:** Create daily habits that consciously connect you to God's all-sufficient love. This might include declaring specific truths about His nature and your identity, practicing gratitude for evidence of His provision, or intentionally receiving care from others as an expression of divine love through human channels.

Made in the USA
Coppell, TX
10 March 2025

46938533R00098